MARRIAGE

JPS Popular Judaica Library
General Editor: Raphael Posner

MARRIAGE

Edited by Hayyim Schneid

JEWISH PUBLICATION SOCIETY OF AMERICA
Philadelphia, Pa.

Copyright © Israel Program for Scientific Translations Ltd., 1973

First published in Israel by KETER BOOKS, an imprint of
ISRAEL PROGRAM FOR SCIENTIFIC TRANSLATIONS LTD.
P.O. Box 7145, Jerusalem

Published by
THE JEWISH PUBLICATION SOCIETY OF AMERICA
222 N. 15th St., Philadelphia, Pa. 19102

Library of Congress Catalogue Card 72 13536
ISBN 0 8276 0013 5
All rights reserved

Manufactured by Keter Press, Jerusalem, Israel 1973

Printed in Israel

CONTENTS

INTRODUCTION

One of the striking aspects of the social revolution that has been in progress since the second world war in most of the western world has been the change in the attitude to sex. Sex has, so to speak, come out into the open; Victorianism and Puritanism have disappeared. The subject is treated openly and in detail in the press and on the screen; books are published that only a couple of decades ago would have been banned by the censor. The lyrics to many of the popular songs would have made people's hair stand on edge only twenty-five years ago and dress habits have changed radically. All these manifestations point to greater sexual freedom than perhaps has been known before and of course the discovery of the "pill" has helped it along.

Very few people would want the world to return to the Victorian era and its stifling suppression—indeed it has been suggested that the present "explosion" is a delayed reaction to just that era. Most serious people would agree that a subject as important as sex should be treated openly and frankly and that society's mental health depends, to a great extent, on such a treatment. However, most people would also agree that things have gone too far. It is hard not to associate the general breakdown we are witnessing in our modern society with attitudes toward sex—and we do seem to be witnessing such a breakdown. Often, hands are thrown up in despair at a situation over which we seem to have no control.

Perhaps one of the most disturbing elements in the whole business is the deterioration of the parent-child relationship. One often hears statements like "What the hell! the world's going to pot! Why! Kids cannot even talk to their parents any more." But surely it should be just the opposite way around: The world's going to pot *because* children cannot talk to their parents any more. The family is the basic unit of our society and it is to the family that one must look for the cause of the "pot" and, hopefully its correction.

In discussing the family itself the starting point is, very simply, the mother and father. Those two people joined together to create the family; they conceived and bore the children; they brought them up and they served as their example. Most observers of the present day scene would agree that one of our major problems is the relationship between father and mother. The confusion caused by mixing the parental roles is often pointed to by psychologists as one of the main causes for emotional disturbances in children—and thus in adults. The father who is too "soft" and the mother who "wears the pants" rarely, if ever, understand that the swopping of roles is, to say the least, not the most healthy climate for the kids to grow up in.

To see society we must look at its basic unit, the family and to see the family we must look at the husband and wife. The purpose of this book is to present the traditional Jewish view of the subject and also to provide information about the various laws and ceremonies with their accompanying customs. Obviously it is impossible to treat the subject anywhere near comprehensively in a book of this nature but an attempt is made to present the main facets, and that on a popular level. For the benefit of readers who wish to pursue the subject, the main sources are provided at the end of the book as is an English language bibliography.

Western attitudes are based, to a large degree, on Jewish tradition. Some modern religious thinkers describe the western ethic as Judeo-Christian. This is particularly true in the attitudes to sex; the degrees of incestuous relationship commonly accepted in the western world are, by and large, based on the Old Testament; polyandry (wife sharing) is generally condemned; marriage is still seen as the ideal state and seems to be accepted as natural. After all, even in the great Bolshevic revolution the "glass of water" attitude to sex was soon abandoned and marriage as an institution took over again. It should be of value, therefore, to see how rabbinic Judaism developed the idea of marriage and defined the marriage relationship. The traditional Jewish attitude is best reflected in the *halakhah* (Jewish law) and the customs that have grown up around it and from a reading of that material one can come to understand the motivation, often not articulated, that inspired its creation.

One often hears the question "Is Jewish law and tradition relevant to the modern man? The world has changed and so have human values." The question is, of course, a very valid one and indeed a person with even a nodding acquaintance with history can bolster it immensely. After all the rabbis of the Talmud lived nearly two thousand years ago in, by modern technological standards, a primitive society—how can what they said mean anything to us today?

However, what is relevant to us today? Are we prepared to accept the dehumanization of the human being of, say, Orwell's "1984" society? Surely, our present problems really stem from our unwillingness to accept the destination we seem to be headed for. Thus everything should be relevant to us in our quest for a better and more meaningful life and particularly the thought and ethic of a group of men who were mainly concerned with the human being as a human being and his relationship to God. All human beings are the product of their history and it surely behooves us to know how our ancestors addressed themselves to the problem of being a human being. To understand the attitude of the rabbis properly entails a great deal of training in the discipline and a tremendous amount of study. This book is presented to help the reader who does not have that training to achieve, at least, a minimum knowledge of the subject in order for it to be a factor in his own thinking.

Marriage benedictions, from Rothschild Miscellany 24, N. Italy, c. 1470.

1. SEX AND MARRIAGE

Judaism is a religious system relevant to every aspect of life. Man's sexual urge is one of the most, if not the most, fundamental part of his nature. Judaism would not go so far as some modern schools of psychology to say that the sex instinct is the basic formulative factor but it does recognize the crucial role that that instinct plays in human existence and, as such, legislates for it. Neither the Bible nor the rabbis considered the sex act to be intrinsically sinful or shameful, but rather a legitimate human activity which when performed properly achieves the status of a *mitzvah*. Were it not for that instinct, the rabbis state, "no man would build a home or marry," and it was with the sex urge in mind, the Midrash relates, that the creation of the world was completed and God pronounced His work as "very good."

In primitive religions, the holy is considered an intrinsic, impersonal, *The Holy* neutral quality inherent in objects, persons, rites and sites; a power charged with contagious efficacy and, therefore, taboo. Seldom is this quality of holiness ascribed to the deity. In Judaism, however, holiness expresses the very nature of God and it is He who is its ultimate source and who is denominated the Holy One. Objects, persons, sites and activities that are employed in the service of God derive their sacred character from that relationship; the intention with which an act is performed, together with the way in which it is performed, determines its sanctity. The law sets down the guidelines and, because of its divine sanction, those deeds performed in accordance with the law become holy.

The possibility of holiness applies to the sexual relationship of man and woman as well. Of interest is the Pentateuchal commentators' interpretation of the command "you shall be holy, for I the Lord your God am holy," as referring to the holiness attained by self-control in sexual behavior. The mode of attaining self-control, as explained, is through marriage.

1

In this, the Jewish view of chastity is quite different from the classical Christian view. Jewish chastity is not an avoidance of sex but the avoidance of illicit sex. Sex is not evil—embodied in Original Sin, incompatible with the holiness required of a priest or a nun, and for others a concession to human frailty—but a legitimate good, even a *mitzvah*. Similarly, Judaic thought cannot agree that procreation is the only justification for the sex act. Independent of procreation, the husband's conjugal obligations are to be carried out with a certain frequency and with the aim of strengthening mutual affection; they continue during the wife's pregnancy or if she is barren. However, the rabbis pointed to the verse "He created it [the world] not a waste, he formed it to be inhabited" as the source for the religious duty not only of marrying but of setting up a family. The Mishnah sees procreation as the fulfillment of the command "be fruitful and multiply," the minimum number of children being two (according to Bet Shammai two male children; according to Bet Hillel one male and one female).

When the procreational *mitzvah* must be set aside, for example for health reasons, proper contraception is called for by the various rabbinic responsa. In choosing a means of contraception one must consider several factors. Under no circumstances does *halakhah* permit male contraception: The Bible records that Er and Onan were killed by God for having "spilled their seed" when they married, one after the other, their dead brother's wife, Tamar. This is understood to mean that they practiced *coitus interruptus* in order not to "raise up seed for their brother" (see page 49); this is the most unnatural method of frustrating the performance of the *mitzvah*. Emphasis must be placed on the naturalness of the sexual union. Whereas various irregular forms of sexual play are permitted in Jewish law, the more normal form is favored. Similarly, the more natural the form of contraception the less objectionable it would be considered. This is as opposed to abstinence, which is rejected as an unwarranted frustration of the marital *mitzvah* and thus unnatural.

Chastity, then is the manner in which Judaism steers a course between the excesses of promiscuity and puritanism.

2

This insistence on "naturalness" seems to be a decisive factor in the Jewish attitude to sex. The Bible already forbids outright such unnatural practices as homosexuality, bestiality, and sodomy. Reference is made in the Bible to "the abominations of Egypt" which certainly means the depraved sexual practices of that country at that time. Emphasis is placed on the man and woman fulfilling their natural role as such; a man is forbidden to wear female clothing and *vice versa*. The laws of family purity (see page 64) would tend to stress the femininity of the woman.

Rabbinic *halakhah* knew of persons who were abnormal sexually from a biological point of view and legislated for the hermaphrodite and the person of undeterminable sex (the *androgynus* and the *tumtum* respectively). The Midrash takes the verse "Male and female He created them" of the Creation story as referring to the creation of a single individual. Whereas Jeremiah ben Eleazar explains that it refers to the creation of an *androgynos*, Samuel ben Nahman suggests that the verse means "He created them with a double face which was then severed in two." This indicates that the sages were well aware of the bisexual nature of man and used it to explain the existence of sexual deviates. However, the rabbis would never have accepted such an explanation as justifying "abnormal" or "deviate" sexual behavior.

Masturbation is not expressly forbidden in the Bible although there are opinions which derive such a prohibition by analogy from the story of Er and Onan notwithstanding the obvious ingredient of malicious intent in that story. Jewish mystical tradition, which frequently uses the sexual act in its theosophic allegories, treats masturbation as a sin whose perpetration causes the removal of the Divine Presence from Israel. This attitude is presumably based on the idea of "naturalness" and the horrifying thought—to the mystical mind—of wasting the material out of which life is formed. It should be remembered that one of the main purposes of the Kabbalah is to explain the act of Creation. From the mystical tradition the prohibition is taken up by many—but not all—halakhic authorities.

3

It is quite apparent that Judaism's view on celibacy also differs greatly from the Christian view. Rabbinic teaching sees celibacy as unnatural. It is not he who marries who sins; the sinner is the unmarried man who does not fulfill the command "be holy" and thus indiscriminately succumbs to his sexual urge or spends his days in sinful thoughts. Furthermore, according to some sages, celibacy is almost a punishable crime: he who fails to marry and produce children "is as if he shed blood, diminished the image of God, and made the *Shekhinah* depart from Israel," and he will have to account for his actions in the world to come.

It is significant that the choice of the Hebrew term for marriage is *kid-* *dushin,* a word derived from the root KDŠ—to be holy. By the act of marriage a man sanctifies his existence.

Marriage also fulfills the individual as a person: "He who has no wife is not a proper man"; he lives "without joy, blessing, goodness . . . and peace"; he may not officiate as high priest on the Day of Atonement, and, ideally, not as *ḥazzan* on the High Holy Days.

Because marriage is in compliance with God's will, it is no wonder that God Himself is portrayed, in Jewish literature, as the grand matchmaker. A story is told of a Roman woman who, upon hearing from Rabbi Yose ben Ḥalafta that the world was created in six days, asked what God had been doing since that time. Rabbi Yose answered that God was occupied with matchmaking, proclaiming before their birth whose daughter would marry whom. Although this might appear to be an easy task, he said, in God's eyes it was as difficult as the dividing of the Red Sea. In an attempt to outdo the Creator, the lady thereupon paired off in marriage a thousand male slaves with a thousand slave-girls. Her success was shortlived. After only one night, all the slaves protested that theirs was a poor match. She understood that Rabbi Yose had been right and that marriages are indeed arranged in heaven.

The story of Jacob and Rachel in the Bible clearly indicates the acceptance of romantic love as an ingredient in marriage and the various talmudic and midrashic accounts of Rabbi Akiva's marriage seem to suggest that marriage for love is the ideal. In that case, Akiva, the ignoramus, became, through his love, the most renowned of the great sages.

The imagery used in the Bible and in later sources for the relationship of God to Israel is also based on the love of a man for a woman. Indeed, the theme of the biblical Song of Songs, which the rabbis described as the "holiest of holies," is romantic love.

In the Bible the view that marriage is the perfect state and a sanctified *God Married* rite is taken to extremes. God is described as being married to His people *to Israel* Israel, a relationship conceived in holiness and contracted to outlast even the end of days. God Himself utters, "and I will betroth thee (Israel) unto Me forever. Yea, I will betroth thee unto Me in righteousness, and in justice, and in lovingkindness, and in compassion. And I will betroth thee unto Me in faithfulness; and thou shalt know the Lord." Isaiah, in speaking of Israel's return to God, and God's return to His people at the

A Jew with his bride, the blindfolded "synagoga."

5

end of days, can find no better analogy than marriage: "For as a young man espouseth a virgin, so shall thy sons espouse thee; and as the bridegroom rejoiceth over the bride, so shall thy God rejoice over thee." Similarly, the rabbis use marriage to symbolize other perfect relationships: e.g., Israel and the Torah; Israel and the Sabbath.

As marriage was not to be taken lightly, Jewish thought concerns itself *Choosing a* with every detail. A man may even sell a Torah Scroll in order to marry *Partner* and the sages believe that a woman will often tolerate an unhappy marriage rather than remain alone. Choosing a bride requires much deliberation. Marriage should not be for money, and a man should seek a wife who is mild-tempered, tactful, modest and industrious and who meets other criteria: beauty, similarity of social background and of age, respectability of family, and having a scholarly father. A man should not betroth a woman until he has gotten to know her. Early marriage is preferred: "eighteen for marriage." If a man is not married by twenty some scholars allow courts of law to force him to marry, while others say that God curses him. Only a person intensively occupied in Torah study may postpone marriage; though some scholars suggest that one should first marry and then study. A practical order of procedure derived from the Bible states: "First build a house, then plant a vineyard, and after that marry."

Although marriage is considered a sacred relationship, it is not a sacra- *Sacred vs.* ment in the Christian sense; its dissolution through divorce is possible, *Sacrament* though regrettable. Marriage is effected through a legal contract; it must, however, not be devoid of spiritual content, i.e., both parties must seek to raise their marriage to the highest level by means of mutual consideration and respect.

In Hebrew, both the word for a man, אִישׁ, and that for a woman, אִשָּׁה, are *Marriage, God's* composed of three letters, two of which are identical: אשׁ—meaning fire. *Presence and* The additional letters represent God's name. Thus, the Talmud explains, *Fire* when a man and woman live together harmoniously they add the presence of the Almighty to their marriage; however, if their marriage is unhappy the only common factor is the presence of a consuming fire.

6

Bukharan bridal
gown of cotton tulle
with Jewish motifs
in the embroidery.

רחל דר חאל וסמה כשידן

Painting of a bride from Persia with inscription in Judeo-Persian indicating that she is applying a blue cosmetic to her eyes, late 18th century. (see also plate 3)

Therefore, by way of advice, a husband is told to deny himself in order to provide for his wife and children: "a man should spend less than his means on food, up to his means on clothes, beyond his means in honoring wife and children." He must also not cause his wife to weep, and if he loves her as himself and honors her more than himself, he will merit the blessing "and thou shalt know that thy tent is in peace."

Just as the rabbis realized the difficulties inherent in successful match-making, they understood the problem of maintaining the marriage relationship. Jewish law, therefore, carefully defined the rights and obligations of both the husband and wife in order to avoid the fears and uncertainties which accompany an undefined relationship. Only in a clear, secure and content relationship can both parties to the marriage make their best contribution to it. The act of marriage, the wedding ceremony, is thus a combination of a religious ceremony and a legal contract designed to send off the couple on their long voyage through life together. *Rights and Obligations*

2. THE WEDDING

The marriage ceremony has undergone many changes and borne many additions throughout the ages; and even nowadays, although the basic elements are the same in the rites of all communities, there are still different customs which often reflect the different cultural backgrounds of the communities.

Being a central event in the life cycle, the actual wedding ceremony was, and is, both preceded and followed by many minor ceremonies and customs. Some of these are customs which originated in a fear of the evil eye or evil spirits and are designed to protect the couple; others are acts intended to invoke blessings on the couple, particularly the blessing of fertility. In the course of time the sources for these customs have been forgotten and other homiletical explanations have been supplied; they remain, however, colorful components of the cycle of getting married. *Customs*

7

There is hardly any data about the marriage ceremony in the Bible. The act of marriage is called simply "taking" ("when a man taketh a wife"; "and there went a man of the house of Levi, and he took a daughter of Levi"). However, from the story of Jacob and Leah it is obvious that some

Jacob's wives, Rachel and Leah. From a 15th century French manuscript.

Eliezer, Abraham's servant, meeting Rebecca at the well (Genesis 24: 15) and being taken to her parent's home. From a 6th century Byzantine manuscript.

sort of celebration did take place: "And Laban gathered all the people of the place and made a feast" and later, when Jacob complained that he had been cheated and demanded Rachel, the daughter for whom he had worked, he was told: "fulfill the (bridal) week of this one, and we will give thee the other also." No details are recorded as to the nature of the feast or the bridal week. The same is true in the case of Samson except that there it is said that the groom posed a riddle to his companions and gave them seven days of the feast to solve it. It appears that processions for both the bride and groom were a central part of the celebrations and were accompanied by music and there is ample reference to special marriage attire and adornment. It also seems that the exhibition of evidence of the bride's virginity (the blood-stained sheet) was part of the ceremony. It is reasonable to assume that even in the earliest times the act of marriage must have been accompanied by some ceremony; the Bible, how-

9

ever, gives no direct description of it and usually refers to it only in passing or as a figure of imagery.

In talmudic times (and presumably even prior to it) the marriage act *Erusin and* consisted of two parts. The first, called *erusin* or *kiddushin* (betrothal), *Nissu'in* was followed a year later in the case of a virgin and thirty days later in other cases by *nissu'in* (marriage). After the betrothal ceremony the couple were to all intents and purposes married except that they did not cohabit and the husband was not yet required to support his wife. The marriage ceremony consisted of bringing the bride to the groom's home after which cohabitation took place. During the Middle Ages both ceremonies began to be performed together in order to eliminate a situation in which the bride was married but did not live with her husband, a situation which, particularly in unsettled times, could lead to many serious problems. At present, the two ceremonies are separated only by the reading of the *ketubbah*.

3. BEFORE THE WEDDING DAY

The choosing of a marital partner was either arranged by parents, rela- *Choosing* tives, a marriage broker (known as a *shadkhan*) or the couple themselves. Although the Bible does not describe in detail how marriages were arranged, it does relate that Abraham instructed his servant Eliezer to find a wife for Isaac. Jacob, on the other hand, chose his own wife. In talmudic times, marriages were often arranged by the heads of two families with no broker involved.

The term *shadkhan* in its present meaning first appears in rabbinic litera- *Shadkhan* ture in the 13th century, where the question as to whether the broker should receive his fee even if the marriage does not take place is discussed. Originally, the matchmaking profession was highly esteemed and many famous rabbis earned their livelihood as such. In the Middle Ages, rabbis and scholars were the natural go-between because fathers were anxious to secure learned and pious sons-in-law. In time, however, the traditional **10** integrity of the profession began to decline. Men with unstable backgrounds and occupations ventured into the profession's uncertain undertakings. The peculiar talents required stimulated the development of a unique type of personality; generally, the *shadkhan* could be relied upon to be a perpetual chatterbox, good-natured and sometimes even a gross exaggerator.

The most common occurrence in modern times is for the couple themselves to do the choosing. Similarly, in ancient Israel, the Mishnah records, on two days of the year—on the fifteenth of the month of Av and on the Day of Atonement—unmarried girls would dress in white and go out to the fields where the men were waiting to choose them as brides. Although other methods of matchmaking were employed throughout the year, these two occasions became the most festive and cherished days of the calendar.

A Jewish engagement by a 19th century non-Jewish artist, Herman Junkker.

An embroidery made by Elizabeth Judah, aged 17 from Montreal, in 1777, as a marriage gift for her future husband, Judah Myers, of Norfolk, Virginia.

In very early times the engagement of a man and woman was made a for- *Tena'im*
mal ceremony known as *shiddukhin*. At this ceremony the terms of the
marriage were formulated. It was sometimes customary to reduce the
conditions *(tena'im)* of the *shiddukhin* to writing. This document (see page
97) would include the date and place of the proposed marriage, and the
financial obligations of the parties, i.e., the dowry to be brought by the
bride, or the period for which her father undertook to provide for the
couple.

The conditions undertaken varied according to location. By talmudic *Dowry*
times, the minimum dowry the father gave his daughter was the equivalent of 180 grams of silver, but larger amounts were quite usual. In the
case of an orphan, the brothers were required to provide the dowry from
the inheritance. An extremely poor girl was provided for by community

A niello Key casket, probably given as a wedding gift to a bride. Ferrara (?)
Italy, c. 1470. The front is decorated with illustrations of the three commandments, incumbent on a woman: setting aside a portion of the dough *(hallah)*,
ritual immersion and kindling the Sabbath lights.

13

Embroidered velvet cover for a frontdoor *mezuzah*, given by a bride to her future husband. The silver thread embroidery includes the bride's name—Simḥah Hamou. Morocco, 19th century.

funds collected for that purpose. In some communities, the groom's parents equalled the bride's father's gift.

The amount of the dowry was recorded in the marriage contract *(ketubbah)* which in present practice usually stipulates one aggregate sum which includes the monetary equivalent of the dowry. Upon a childless wife's death the dowry belonged to the husband; however, in order to stimulate her father to provide a greater amount, a 12th-century enactment made the dowry returnable in toto to the father should his daughter die

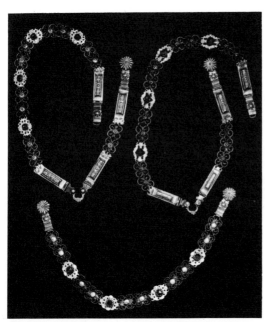

Pair of marriage belts with chain to link the bride to the groom. Belts of this type were the most distinctive wedding gift in Germany during the 17th century.

14

childless in the first year of marriage; if she died in the second year without children, one half was to be returned. In 1761 a rabbinical conference modified these rules; the husband received, upon her death, the complete dowry only after five years of childless marriage.

Dowry was the accepted custom in Ashkenazi communities to the exclusion of *mohar* (bride-price), a biblical custom in common practice among the Jews of Muslim countries. *Mohar* consisted of the payment of 50 *shekels* to the bride's father by the groom. Very often, the father used this money to buy necessities for the couple. In addition, it was customary for the groom to give the bride gifts and in return she would bring certain properties to his home upon marriage: slaves, cattle, real estate, etc. *Mohar*

Whatever the case, all the stipulations were binding and often a penalty was agreed upon in the event of breach of promise without good cause. In addition to this penalty the party committing the breach may also have been liable to compensate for actual damage sustained, such as expenses of preparation and the returning of gifts received from relatives and friends. The procedure for releasing the parties from their agreements was, therefore, delicate and difficult. It was not uncommon for rabbis to suggest that the wedding take place (if this satisfied the conditions) and thereafter issue a divorce. *Breach of Promise*

The *tena'im* ceremony is only in partial practice today. Although it loses its significance, it is sometimes performed just prior to the wedding ceremony to preclude any possibility of breach. Another reason for the preservation of this ceremony, although it has no immediate effect on the personal status of the parties—it being only a promise to create a different personal status in the future—is the fact that the talmudic sages regarded marriage without *shiddukhin* as licentious. *Tena'im Today*

When performed, the Ashkenazi ceremony ends with the breaking of a plate; an act parallel to the crushing of a glass at the wedding ceremony.

The period from the close of the engagement ceremony until the final week before the wedding was marked by preparations for the festivities. *Gifts*

15

In addition, in some communities the future bride and groom exchanged gifts, known as *sivlonot*. For example, in Oriental countries, on Passover, Shavuot, and Sukkot, the groom would send his fiancée clothing, jewelry and choice fruits. An Ashkenazi groom might send clothing or jewelry to his future bride and she would reciprocate with a new *tallit* (prayer shawl) or *tallit* bag she had made herself. The Bulgarian Romaniots regarded the sending of gifts as part of the wedding, and, if later, the marriage did not take place a divorce was required.

On the Sabbath prior to the wedding ceremony the groom is given the honor of being called to the reading of the Torah, when he is showered with rice, wheat, nuts and candy—a fertility symbol from which the modern confetti derives. This custom, known among Ashkenazim as *aufrufen*, is preceded in some communities by the recital of special hymns. The groom is similarly honored on the Sabbath following his wedding. In some communities, on this occasion the groom is seated in a place of honor with a ceremonial canopy spread above him. In Libya and Tunisia, a second Torah scroll is taken out and an additional section read in his honor. Traditionally, on the Sabbaths both immediately before and after his wedding the bridegroom is the first who has a right to be called to the Torah, with precedence even over a bar-mitzvah boy. *Aufrufen*

In view of the prohibition on a man to have relations with his menstruous wife (during her menses and for a period of seven "clean" days thereafter; see page 64), it is obligatory for the future bride to immerse herself in the *mikveh* (ritual bath) on one of the evenings prior to the marriage. If this is not permissible, i.e., she has not completed the required time limit since her last menses, a slight modification in the wedding takes place and she then immerses herself at the earliest possible time. Whereas normally a woman goes to the *mikveh* alone out of modesty, in most instances a bride is permitted to have another woman accompany her to the *mikveh* for her first immersion. In some Sephardi communities, festivities accompany the bride's emergence from the waters of the *mikveh*. *Mikveh*

16

Jewess immersing herself in a *mikveh* before going to her husband, who awaits her in bed (left). Yemenite bride smearing henna on her father's finger (right).

It is usual for the bride and groom to refrain from seeing each other for some time preceding the wedding. The actual duration of this period varies in the different communities from about one week to one day, i.e., that of the wedding itself until the ceremony. *Meeting before the Wedding*

In some Ashkenazi communities the bride (sometimes the groom as well), if she is an orphan, visits the grave of her parents in the week prior to the wedding. *Visiting the Cemetery*

In Tunisia the groom is invited to the bride's home on the Sabbath preceding the wedding and has to find a roast chicken which has been especially hidden. In Cochin, at the conclusion of the Sabbath, the future bride is escorted in procession to her sister's or relative's home where she remains until the wedding.

In most Oriental communities the *ḥinnah* is celebrated the night before the wedding. In this ceremony the women of both families and female *Ḥinnah*

17

friends (men are usually excluded) gather at the home of the bride and paint the bride's hands with red henna. This ceremony is either a symbol of the bride's virginity (it is not performed for a widow or a divorcée) or intended to ward off the evil eye and is sometimes accompanied by a ceremonial compounding of the dye by the bride's mother and feeding the bride seven times during the evening.

In some communities (Afghanistan and, in a modified form, Yemen) it was sometimes customary to arrange a private wedding ceremony the night before the announced day. On the morrow the announced ceremony would also be held. This was in order to outwit evil spirits or malicious persons who wished to cast spells on the couple.

As marriage is viewed as the beginning of a new era in the life of the couple and they receive atonement for all their past transgressions, it is customary for the couple to add the confessional liturgy of the Day of Atonement to the afternoon service before the ceremony.

4. THE WEDDING DAY

The marriage ceremony is one of Judaism's most festive traditions, being the commencement of man's life as a complete person. The choice of a wedding day, therefore, requires careful deliberation. *Choosing the Day*

Although not obligatory, some rabbis recommend that the couple marry in the first half of the lunar month while the moon is waxing, as a sign of blessing.

Whereas it is customary for the couple to fast on their wedding day as part of their atonement for past transgressions, many couples choose *rosh hodesh* (the first day of the lunar month) except that of the month of Nisan, the eight days of Hanukkah (some scholars require the couple to fast on the fourth day), the fifteenth of Av or the fifteenth of Shevat, which are minor festivals, or the day following Shavuot for the ceremony since it is forbidden to fast on those days. *Fasting*

A Wednesday *Ketubbah* from Gibraltar, 1872.

The Mishnah ruled that a virgin should marry on Wednesday. One ex- *Blessing of* planation for this is the fact that the court sat on Thursdays and thus if *Creation* the groom claimed that his bride had not been a virgin he could immediately complain. The Mishnah also ruled that a widow should marry on Thursday so that her husband should devote at least three days to her, Thursday, Friday, and the Sabbath, without going back to his work. Another explanation, based on the biblical account of Creation, connects these days with blessings particularly appropriate for the bride and groom, such as, the fertility blessing of Thursday: "Be fruitful and multiply, and fill the waters in the seas, and let fowl multiply in the earth." These requirements, even in talmudic times, fell into disuse. Some Orthodox couples are careful to choose Tuesday because of the repetition of the phrase "and God saw that this was good" in the Creation story. In modern times, especially in the western hemisphere, Sunday is the most popular day because of the convenience it affords the guests.

On the other hand, the marriage ceremony is prohibited, for various reasons, on certain days.

Because one is not permitted to mix one festivity with another, but must *Festivals* enjoy each for itself, marriages are not performed on any of the major festivals (i.e., Rosh ha-Shanah, Passover, Shavuot, and Sukkot) or their intermediate days. For the same reason, some rabbinic scholars prohibit marriages on Purim and this is the prevalent custom today.

Marriages are not performed on the Sabbath or Day of Atonement be- *Sabbath* cause the legal aspects of the ceremony constitute a desecration of that day's sanctity.

One may not marry during a period of national mourning as personal *Mourning* joy would then be unseemly. Thus, marriage is prohibited from the seventeenth of the month of Tammuz up to, and including, the ninth of the month of Av (the anniversary of the destruction of both Temples in Jerusalem), and according to custom during part of the *omer* period (i.e., the 49 days) between Passover and Shavuot (the period normally as- **20** sociated with a plague that took many of the lives of the disciples of Rabbi Akiva). One custom concerning this period, for example, prohibits marriages from the first day of the month of Iyyar until the end of the *omer* period (Shavuot), while another custom begins the prohibition with the beginning of the period (Passover) and ends it with the thirty-third day of the *omer* (i.e., Lag ba-Omer). In the State of Israel, Lag ba-Omer is a very festive day and one of the most popular for weddings.

According to talmudic law if on the wedding day the father of the groom or the mother of the bride should die, the funeral is set aside until after the wedding is celebrated. The couple begin their period of mourning only after the seven days of the marriage festivities. In any other case of death whereby either bride or groom becomes a mourner, the funeral takes place immediately after which follow seven days of mourning and then the wedding is celebrated. However, later authorities rule that the wedding is postponed even in the former case.

Many communities have instituted their own customs based on local culture; for example, the Falasha community does not perform weddings during the entire month of Nisan and during the rainy season in Ethiopia (July through September).

There are no specific requirements for the way in which the bride and *Dress* bridegroom dress. However, it has become customary for the bride to wear white, as a sign of purity, and for her to have a headdress and veil. The Mishnah already records the custom of *hinnoma* which has been *Veil* interpreted to mean the veil a virgin bride wore. In the 15th century Rhineland, the bridal veil was always a gift from the bridegroom, and in the 17th/18th centuries some communities forbad the wearing of gold or spun gold on the veil. However, in 19th century Tunisia, Jewish brides often wore gold embroidered veils. In certain ḥasidic circles, brides have their faces completely wrapped and covered.

In some Orthodox circles the bridegroom wears a *kitel* (white gown) either as an evocation of death or since his wedding day is compared to the Day of Atonement when the *kitel* is worn. Some grooms wear the

An engraving of a veiled bride escorted by two women wearing the typical costume of the period. Fuerth, Germany 1705.

An orthodox bride from Mea Shearim, Jerusalem, wearing a double veil, which entirely covers her face.

marriage *kitel* as an inner garment that cannot be seen. The bridegroom, and in some communities the officiating rabbi, also wears a *tallit*.

In some Oriental communities brides wear elaborate costumes, richly embroidered and ornamented, which are borrowed for the occasion. The bride sometimes also wears jewelry; in talmudic times she wore as a diadem a "city of gold" (representing Jerusalem) such as Rabbi Akiva once gave his wife.

Painting of a groom from Persia with Judeo-Persian inscription indicating that he is playing a *tar*, late 18th century. (see also plate 2)

Painting of a bride
in East European
wedding garments.
Isidor Kaufmann
(1853–1921).

Wedding rings
from Italy (top left,
bottom middle
and right), Austria
(bottom left), and
North Africa (top
right), 17th and
18th centuries.

An orthodox bridegroom wearing a *kitel*, awaits his bride under the *huppah*
(left). A Yemenite groom in Israel, wearing a *tallit*, as the officiating rabbi
reads the *ketubbah* (right). An etching of a wedding ceremony being conducted
outside the synagogue. Germany c. 1720 (below).

AA

A contemporary wedding inside the Shaar Hashomayim synagogue in Montreal.

Site The ceremony may be performed anywhere. In many communities—particularly Sephardi and Oriental—it is performed inside the synagogue, although there are contrary halakhic opinions. In some places it is performed in the open. This latter custom is perhaps due to the fact that ideally the ceremony takes place after nightfall and the stars above are associated with God's assurances to Abraham that He would "make your descendants as numerous as the stars of Heaven."

Rabbi In order to avoid irregularities which might possibly bring about legal complications, custom decrees that the marriage be solemnized by a competent rabbi. The presence of a rabbi is not, however, essential and a ceremony performed correctly will be valid even if no clergyman is present. It is also generally accepted that there shall be present at least a *minyan* (ten men), to ensure that the marriage act receives maximum publicity.

Ketubbah In modern times, the marriage ceremony begins with the writing of the *ketubbah* (marriage contract), a custom that dates back to the first century B.C.E. Theretofore, the bridegroom simply designated money to be

24

set aside for his wife upon the dissolution of the marriage. To protect the wife's interests, the present form of written contract was instituted (see page 95).

Because it is forbidden for the bridegroom to cohabit with his bride until he has written and delivered the *ketubbah,* and because, at the same time, they are allowed to cohabit only after marriage (i.e., *nissu'in*), the

Ketubbah from
Damascus, 1872.

בסימנא טבא ◆ ובמזלא מעליא

משה כשבת אחד עשר יום לחדש סיון שנת חמשה אלפים וארבע מאות ושלשים
לבריאת עולם למנין שאנו מנין פה פֿערארה הכחור כמר משה יצ'ו כמר שמחה
לוצאטו זל אמר לה להדא כתולתא מרת לאאירא מכת בת כמר משה אלטרייני יצ'ו
הוי לי לאנתו כדת משה וישראל ואנא אפלה ואוקיר ואזון ואפרנס יתיכי כהלכת
גוברין יהודאין דפלחין ומוקירין וזנין ומפרנסין לנשיהון בקושטא ויהיבנא ליכי מהר
בתוליכי כסף זוזי מאתן דחזו ליכי ומזוניכי וכסותיכי וספוקיכי ומיעל לותיכי כאורח כל
ארעא ויצבאת מרת לאאירא מכת דא מכת והות לה לאנתו ולכמר משה יצ'ו
חתן דנן וזן נדוניא דהנעלת ליה לבי אבוה אלף וחמש מאות דיק לעד עשה
ליט ארבעה סולדי דיק מטבע ויצ'אה בכך בעת כחושטיא וחמש מאות דיק לעד
דיק לעד דיק הנל בכך בדברי ומלבושים צעפים ותכשיטים השייכים לגופה וצבי
כמר משה יצ'ו חתן דנן והוסיף לה מן דיליה ממונניא חמש מאות דיק לעד
נמצא סך הכל בין נדוניא ותוספתא אא שני אלפים וחמש מאות דיק לעד
הנל עם המאתן וזזי דחזו לה וכך אמר כמר משה יצ'ו חתן דנן אחריות
כתובתא נדוניא ותוספתא דא קבלית עלי ועל ירתאי כתראי להתפרעא מן
כל שפר ארג נכסין וקנינין דאית לי תחות כל שמיא דקנאי ודעתיד אנא למקנא
להון אחריות ואיבן דלית להון אהריות נהון אחראין וערבאין לכל כתובתא
מכוהון כתובתא נדוניא ותוספתא דא ערגמירא ואפי'לו מן גלמיא דעל כתפאי
כדי' ובמיתא מן יומא דנן ולעלם וקבל עליו כמר משה יצ'ו חתן דנן אחריות
וחומר כתובתא נדוניא ותוספתא דא כאוהריות וחומר כל שטרי כתובית דנהיגי
בכנית ישראל אל הכנזלות הצנועות כתיקון חזל דלא כאסמכתא ודלא כטופסי
דשטרי וקנינא מן כמר משה יצ'ו חתן דנן לכמר שמחה לוצאט
זלהתן דנן לפרש לאאירא מכת בת כמר משה אלטרייני יצ'ו הנל בתוליכ דא
קנו שם על כל מאי דכתיב ומפרש לעיל במנא
ב'ה ו ... כשר למקני

Ketubbah from
Yemen, 1774.

ketubbah must be ready for delivery to the bride when the betrothal blessings are recited and before the recital of the marriage blessings. Since in modern times the betrothal and the marriage are celebrated at the same time, the deed must therefore be ready at the commencement of the ceremony.

Ketubbah from Padua, 1670 (opposite).

27

A bridegroom signing the *ketubbah* supervised by officiating rabbi.

Once the *ketubbah* is written, the bridegroom undertakes the obligations therein by a symbolic act of acquisition. This is executed by his taking a piece of cloth, handkerchief, or some other object from the officiating rabbi, lifting it and returning it. The witnesses then sign the document and in many communities the groom also signs. (In some places the act of acquisition and the signing by witnesses is done later during the ceremony when the *ketubbah* is read). *Symbolic Acquisition*

In some Orthodox circles the culmination of the writing of the *ketubbah* is followed by a scholarly discourse delivered by the bridegroom which is customarily repeatedly interrupted by the guests with song and merriment in order to avoid embarrassing bridegrooms who are not capable of preparing such a discourse. A result is that often the groom prepares only the opening paragraph.

In some communities, ashes are placed high up on the forehead of the groom as a symbol of mourning for the destruction of the Temple. *Ashes*

A bridegroom performing the symbolic
act of acquisition by lifting a handkerchief.

The groom is then escorted to the place where the bride is waiting and *Bedeken*
lets down her veil over her face, at which time the rabbi or cantor pro- *di-Kale*
nounces the blessing invoked on Rebekah "O sister be thou the mother
of thousands of ten thousands." This ceremony is known in Yiddish as
bedeken di-kale (covering the bride) and is not practiced by Sephardi
Jews. In some communities the *bedeken* ends with the bride's father
placing his hands above her head as he recites the blessing "May God
make thee as Rachel and Leah."

At this point candles and sometimes torches are lit and carried by the *Candles*
couple's mothers (sometimes fathers as well). One explanation for this
custom, other than the usual warding off of evil spirits, associates the
candles with the thunder and lightning at the revelation at Mount Sinai,
comparing the earthly ties of the human pair with the eternal bondage of
Israel to God and the Torah. A modification of this may be seen in the
Jewish-Italian custom recorded at Pesarro and Modena where the **29**

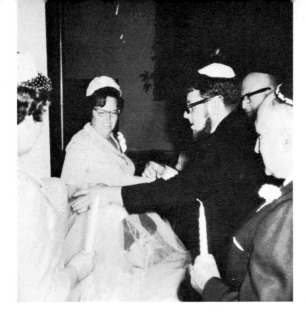

A bridegroom cover-
ing his bride's face
with a veil — *bedeken
di kale.*

bridegroom used to be accompanied by a man carrying a torch to which were attached six more lights, three on each side of the main flame. The allusion is to the seven-branched *menorah* in the Tabernacle and Temple giving the wedding a Jewish-national character.

The groom is then led to the *ḥuppah* (canopy), to the accompaniment *Procession* of music, by his and his bride's father (or two other male relatives or friends if he or the bride has been orphaned) and stands facing Ereẓ Israel, in Israel itself facing Jerusalem, and in Jerusalem facing the

A bride being led
in seven circuits
around the groom
by female relations
holding candles.

30

A bride escorted by women relatives in a candle lit procession.

A kibbutz wedding—the bride and groom are brought to the *huppah* on a tractor-drawn cart.

Temple site. (In some communities, based on Gentile custom, the bridegroom's parents escort the groom as part of a procession beginning with ushers and best man and ending with flower girls, bridesmaids, and the bride with her parents.)

Following the pattern of the groom, the bride is then escorted by her mother and the groom's mother, usually to the accompaniment of a blessing of welcome chanted by the rabbi or cantor, the text of which is: "He who is supremely mighty; He who is supremely praised; He who is supremely great; may He bless this bridegroom and bride."

It is customary among Ashkenazim for the bride to end the procession *Seven Circuits* by being led in seven circuits around the groom, which is presumably to be associated with the magic circle to ward off evil spirits. The bride then stands at the right hand of the groom and the ceremony proper is ready to begin.

In some Oriental communities one of the relatives of the couple holds *Evil Spirits* a pair of scissors and cuts paper or cloth from this point in the ceremony to its conclusion in order to ward off evil spirits. In Kurdistan the officiating rabbi would warn the assembled guests not to cast spells.

The *erusin* (betrothal) begins with the rabbi's recital of the benediction *Betrothal* over a glass of wine followed by the betrothal blessing *(birkat erusin):* "Blessed art Thou, O Lord our God, King of the universe, who has hallowed us by Thy Commandments and has given us command concerning forbidden marriages; who has disallowed unto us those that are betrothed to us, but has sanctioned unto us such as are wedded to us by the rite of the nuptial canopy and the sacred covenant of wedlock. Blessed art Thou, O Lord, who hallowest Thy people Israel by the rite of the nuptial canopy and the sacred covenant of wedlock." The groom and bride are then given to drink from the goblet.

Originally the bridegroom recited these benedictions as well as the seven benedictions of the last part of the ceremony. However, in order not to shame grooms who are unable to make the recitation, it became customary for the officiating persons to recite them all.

32

A groom placing the ring on the forefinger of the bride's right hand.

The groom then places the ring on the forefinger of the bride's right *Ring* hand and recites the marriage formula: *"Harei at mekuddeshet li be-tabba'at zo ke-dat Moshe ve-Yisrael* ("Behold, you are consecrated unto me by this ring, according to the law of Moses and Israel"). For the reason given above it is also customary for the officiating rabbi to pronounce the formula word by word with the groom repeating it after him. This act must be witnessed by two competent individuals who are in no way related to the couple or their families and similarly are not related to each other. They alone may testify to that which occurred, to the exclusion of everyone else even those who did in fact witness the transaction. Should no such competent witnesses be present the marriage act will not be valid.

In Gruzia (Russian Georgia) the transfer of the ring took on a slight modification, i.e., the groom would put the wedding ring into the glass of wine after he had drunk from it, give the glass to the bride to drink,

33

extract the ring and then formally present it to her with the above declaration.

Although the act of betrothal can be effected in several ways, it has become the universal Jewish practice to use a ring, except in a very few Oriental communities where a coin is used. The ring, which must belong to the groom, should be free of any precious stones but can be of any material (usually it is of gold or some other precious metal) as long as its value is more than a *perutah,* the smallest denomination of currency in Talmud times. Generally, the groom places the ring on the forefinger of the bride's right hand; there are, however, many varied customs as to which finger may be used. In some Reform and Conservative congregations in the United States the "double ring" ceremony is practiced in which the bride also gives a ring to the groom and recites a marriage formula. Since, according to the *halakhah,* it is the groom who is acquiring the bride, this innovation raises halakhic doubts which, according to some authorities, may even affect the legal validity of the ceremony.

Besides the above method of effecting the betrothal, two other modes exist (both of which have fallen into complete disuse). One method is *shetar*—in the presence of two competent witnesses, the groom hands over to the bride a deed in which is written, besides the names of the parties and the other particulars required, the words, "Behold you are consecrated unto me with this deed according to the Law of Moses and of Israel," and the bride accepts the deed with the intention of thereby becoming his wife. *Betrothal by Deed*

The other mode is *bi'ah*—if a man in the presence of competent witnesses, addresses to a woman the words, "Behold you are consecrated to me with this cohabitation according to the law of Moses and of Israel," and in their presence he takes her into a private place for the purpose of betrothal, she will, upon their cohabitation, be his wife. Although valid, this mode of betrothal was regarded by the rabbis as promiscuous and they decreed that any person employing it should be punished by flogging. *Betrothal by Cohabitation*

34

The *erusin* (betrothal) ceremony has now come to a close and in some
communities (including many in the State of Israel) a glass is crushed *Glass*
under foot by the groom, while in other places this is done only after the
nissu'in (marriage). The breaking of the glass is explained by some authorities as a token of the seriousness desirable in even the most happy

A groom about to break the glass by throwing it into a dish—a depiction by
Bernard Picart, 1721, of a marriage ceremony amongst Portuguese Jews in
Amsterdam.

35

A groom crushing the glass
in a contemporary ceremony
in Israel.

moments; however, the act has become understood over the ages as a sign of mourning for the destruction of the Temple in Jerusalem; it may originally have been to ward off evil spirits. In some communities the bridegroom threw the glass against a special wall *(traustein)* instead of treading on it. In Libya the groom broke the glass when it was full of wine as a sign of plenty.

In some rites the memorial prayer, *El Maleh Raḥamim,* is recited for departed parents if either member of the couple is an orphan.

At this point, in order to separate the *erusin* from the *nissu'in,* the *ketub-* *Ketubbah*
bah is read out loud by the rabbi or some other man whom the bridal *Reading*
couple wish to honor. In many communities it is read in the original Aramaic and followed by a précis in the vernacular; in Israel a Hebrew précis is often substituted. Sometimes the reading is followed by the signing of the *ketubbah* by two witnesses and the act of acquisition by the bridegroom if these had not been done before the ceremony. The *ketubbah* is then handed to the bride. She must be careful never to lose this document because in such a case cohabitation would be forbidden until a new *ketubbah* was drawn up (see page 98).

The last of the major ceremonies is the marriage—sometimes referred to *Marriage*
as *nissu'in* and sometimes as *ḥuppah* (the *ḥuppah* being the mode in which the *nissu'in* is carried out).

36

A groom throwing the glass against a *traustein*, a special stone set into the
synagogue wall. Germany, c. 1720.

In ancient times the *ḥuppah* was a tent or room of the groom into which, *Ḥuppah*
at the end of the betrothal period, the bride was brought in festive procession for the marital union. Later on the *ḥuppah* became a symbolic
canopy sometimes made completely of wood. The talmud records that
the father of the groom was responsible for its construction. In Bethar
(near Jerusalem) the custom was to make the staves or beams of the

huppah from a cedar and pine tree which were planted for this purpose at the birth of the groom and bride respectively. Besides wood, various other materials were used, such as precious scarlet or gold cloth or even an assortment of flowers spread over crossbeams. In the Middle Ages, in France, the groom simply spread his *tallit* over the bride's head as a symbol of his sheltering her. This type of *huppah* was also common in many North African communities. In the late Middle Ages the *huppah*, consisting of a cloth spread on four staves, was placed inside the synagogue, but later it was moved to the courtyard, either because it was deemed improper to marry in the synagogue or because of the need to accommodate the wedding party. In modern Israel, for the weddings of soldiers on active duty, the *huppah* often consists of a *tallit* which is supported by four rifles held by friends of the bride and groom.

Although, in most communities at present, the couple is already under the canopy from before the betrothal, the *huppah* creates the marriage

Groom placing ring on bride's finger. The *huppah* is a *tallit* spread over both of them. Note musicians in foreground. Drawing by Bernard Picart, 1721.

The *ḥuppah* ceremony of Leopold Rothschild and Marie Perugia, London, 1881.

A contemporary *ḥuppah*, Jerusalem, 1960's.

bond only with the pronouncement of the seven benedictions *(sheva berakhot)*. In some communities the couple is led to the *huppah* or the *huppah* is spread above the couple at this point in the ceremony.

The ceremony of seven benedictions begins with the filling of a goblet of wine. The rabbi or some other designated guest then pronounces the blessing over wine followed by six other benedictions *(birkot nissu'in)*. Often, in order to honor several people with participation in the ceremony, each blessing is recited by a different guest. The ceremony ends with the drinking of the wine by groom and bride. *Seven Benedictions*

The six benedictions as recorded in the Talmud, are:

1. Blessed art Thou, O Lord our God, King of the universe, who has created all things to Thy Glory.
2. Blessed art Thou, O Lord our God, King of the Universe, creator of man.
3. Blessed art Thou, O Lord our God, King of the Universe, who has made man in Thine image, after Thy likeness, and has prepared unto him, out of his very self, a perpetual fabric. Blessed art Thou, O Lord, creator of man.
4. May she who was barren (Zion) be exceedingly glad and exult, when her children are gathered within her in joy. Blessed art Thou, O Lord, who makest Zion joyful through her children.
5. O make these loved companions greatly to rejoice, even as of old Thou didst gladden Thy creatures in the Garden of Eden. Blessed art Thou, O Lord, who makest bridegroom and bride to rejoice.
6. Blessed art Thou, O Lord our God, King of the universe, who hast created joy and gladness, bridegroom and bride, mirth and exultation, pleasure and delight, love, brotherhood, peace and fellowship. Soon, O Lord our God, may there be heard in the cities of Judah, and in the streets of Jerusalem, the voice of joy and gladness, the voice of the bridegroom and the voice of the bride, the jubilant voice of bridegrooms from their canopies, and of youths from their feast of song. Blessed art Thou, O Lord, who makest the bridegroom to rejoice with the bride.

A peculiar custom, common in East Europe as well as in Oriental communities was for the bride and groom to attempt to tread on the other's foot at this point in the ceremony, the one who succeeded thus being assured dominance in their life together.

At the conclusion of the *nissu'in* it is customary, if it has not already *Breaking the* been done, for the groom to break a glass, and although it should re- *Glass* sult in sobriety and thoughts about the destruction of the Temple, it usually leads to an eruption of gaiety and song.

Since in talmudic times the *ḥuppah* was the place of marital union and *Yiḥud* therefore required privacy, medieval responsa dealt with the question whether the act of entering the *ḥuppah* was sufficient to constitute marriage or whether it was only to be regarded as a symbol which would still require the couple to retire in privacy. Therefore, in order to avoid doubt, it is required that, in addition to *ḥuppah,* the couple also have the said private meeting. This is done at the conclusion of the marriage ceremony and is known as *yiḥud* (seclusion). The couple in the presence of two witnesses enter a private room and, as this is their first opportunity, they usually break their fasts there. There is no specified time as to how long they must remain secluded and in practice the *yiḥud* lasts no longer than a few minutes. A slight modification takes place if the bride was unable to immerse herself in the *mikveh,* thus making *yiḥud* impossible. In this case a small child enters the private room with the couple and in that way complete privacy is avoided.

Legally bound in matrimony, the husband and wife, amid singing and dancing, now join their guests in a festive meal.

The menu is not restricted by anything other than the usual dietary laws, *Festive Meal* however, in many communities, notably Morocco, fish is always served as a fertility symbol.

The playing of music at the wedding is considered a religious duty. The *Music* ancient custom of playing the flute before the bridal pair has been abandoned but for no apparent reason. Several legends tell of the rabbis' eagerness "to gladden the groom and bride" with song. Often the rabbis themselves would lead the guests in responsorial singing or sometimes alternating choirs of different pitch would sing to the amusement of the couple.

Marriage processions with timbrels and other instruments are mentioned *Dancing* in the Bible and Apocrypha. Song of Songs mentions "a dance of two companies" which may have been a dance performed by the bride on her wedding day while brandishing a sword in her right hand, symbolizing her defence against all suitors but her chosen one.

The scholars of the Talmud ask: "How should one dance before the bride?" In response, several examples are recorded of scholars who danced at weddings as an act of religious devotion. Judah bar Ilai used to take a myrtle twig and dance and sing before the bride. Rabbi Aḥa went as far as to dance with the bride on his shoulders. Samuel bar Rav Isaac, even when he was old, juggled three myrtle twigs as he sang and

A bridegroom slicing the traditional *hallah*, marking the beginning of the festive meal.

42

The banquet at a Yemenite wedding in Israel. Only male guests are present.

danced. At his funeral, a heavenly flame burned above him; a flame that could only be seen once or twice a generation signifying the death of a great man. The rabbis explain that his greatness lay in his enhancing the wedding festivities.

In later periods, dancing in honor of the bride took on a variety of forms and gave rise to the *Mitzvah* dances. In 16th-century Venice the *Mitzvah* dance was as a form of group dance in which the men danced with the bridegroom, and the women with the bride. This conformed with the prevalent practice and the restrictions against mixed dancing in Jewish communities. Later a modified *Mitzvah* dance took form where men took turns to dance with the bride after wrapping something around the hand as a symbol of separation. By the beginning of the 19th century it became the practice for men to dance with the bride while separated

43

Guests dancing around bridal couple in a Jerusalem wedding (left). Woman accompanying the dancing on a tin container at a Yemenite wedding (right).

by a handkerchief held at opposite ends. In the pattern of the *Mitzvah* dance, the bride was usually seated in the middle of a circle of chosen guests while the *baḍhan* (see page 45), serving as master of ceremonies, called each guest by name to step forward and dance with the bride. First honors went to the parents of the couple and to the bridegroom; then scholars and important members of the community took turns. Each would extend to the bride the tip of a handkerchief or receive one from her, then circle with her once or twice to the accompaniment of music from the orchestra. During the wedding festivities guests and neighbors took part in the dancing and even the beggars of the town had the right to dance with the bride. Other dances performed at weddings in East European communities were: *Koilich Tanz*, a dance of salutation to the bride and groom performed by a woman holding a twisted white loaf and some salt to wish them abundance; *Klapper Tanz*, a dance with much handclapping; *Redl, Frailachs, Karahod, Hopke*, vigorous circle dances done by men; *Besem Tanz*, a man dancing with a broom used as horse or musket; *Flash* [Bottle] *Tanz*, a dance with a bottle on the head; *Bobes Tanz* for the grandmothers; *Mechutanem Tanz* for the relatives

44

The bride dancing with one of the guests as shown in *Mitzvah Tanz*, a painting by the 20th century English artist Alva.

of both families; *Broyges Tanz*, a man and a woman portraying quarrel and reconciliation; *Sher, Sherele, Quadrille*, dances based on square and longways dances performed with partners; *Lancelot, Kutzatsky, Bulgar, Pas d'Espagne, Vingerka, Waltz*, forms of popular Russian, Polish, and Rumanian dances. At ḥasidic weddings, an old practice was often revived of dancing in peasant costumes, animal skins, or even Cossack uniforms. Groups of young girls would also dance toward the seated bride from three directions singing *Keizad merakkedim lifnei ha-kallah* ("How should one dance before the bride"). The young men, meanwhile, would dance around the groom. Dancing at the pre-wedding festivities of Yemenite Jews was usually performed by professional women singers and dancers, to the accompaniment of cymbals, drums, and songs without words. It was considered an honor for the women guests to dance with the *mazhera*, a bowl containing the henna dye with which the bride's hands were painted.

The *badḥan* was a common feature at the wedding. He was a professional entertainer who sang folksongs, told comic stories and sometimes parodied portions of the wedding ceremony. At the wedding feast the *badḥan* entertained the guests with music and with jests that contained

Badhan

45

personal allusions to the guests and participants. In recent times, the institution of the *badḥan* has been replaced by more modern forms of entertainment.

The meal concludes with the grace after meals, which is introduced by a *Concluding* special invocation, and is followed by the pronouncement of the same *Seven* seven benedictions that were heard during the ceremony. He who leads *Benedictions* the grace holds a cup of wine; another cup of wine is held in turn by those who pronounce the other six benedictions. Whereas during the ceremony the blessing over the wine preceded the other blessings, the procedure is now reversed. Following the blessing over wine, parts of both cups are poured into an empty glass which is then given to groom and bride to drink.

A Galician *badhan* bringing the wedding party to tears as he sings the bride's praises. An early 20th century Polish postcard.

5. AFTER THE WEDDING DAY

In Jewish tradition, the atmosphere of the marriage festivities should ideally continue for some time after the conclusion of the ceremony. Indeed for a period of one year following the ceremony, the couple remain known as groom and bride. The midrashic passage that the groom is to be compared to a king and should be honored as such applies for this year period.

The wedding festivities of a virgin must last a full week, during which *Duration of* the groom may not leave his bride to go to work even with the bride's *Festivities* permission. In addition, the special invocation to the grace after meals and the seven benedictions which were recited at the wedding feast are similarly recited at every meal of the bride and groom during the festive week provided there are at least ten men at the meal and one of them is a "new face," i.e., somebody who was not present at any previous recitation for the couple. This rule applies to all seven days except the Sabbath, which is itself considered "a new face." All the customs surrounding the seven benedictions at the wedding feast are followed throughout the week (e.g., order of blessings, mixture of wine, etc.). If only three men are present, the last of the six benedictions may be recited. When either member of the couple is celebrating their first marriage the above rules are applied. If, however, both members of the couple are celebrating their second marriage (e.g., widow and widower) the seven benedictions are only said on the first day.

According to the Bible, a betrothed man may not be drafted into the *Army Service* army for fighting and a groom may not be called upon for one year after the marriage for any army duty. These exemptions do not apply in a defensive war. In the State of Israel this law is not followed.

The bride's entry into her new home was marked by many colorful cere- *Entry into* monies. In Libya and Djerba the groom would drop an earthenware *New Home* pitcher of water from the roof and the bride would enter the house by walking through the water and broken pottery. In Jerusalem the

Sephardim used to break a specially baked cake, called *ruska*, above the heads of the bride and groom, while in Baghdad a loaf was cut above the head of the groom. In Afghanistan a fowl was slaughtered to mark the occasion. In Djerba the bride broke open eggs on the doorposts of the house and in Daghestan and Gruzia the doorposts were smeared with butter and honey. In Salonika the groom would stand at the head of the stairs when the bride first entered the house and scatter sweet-meats, rice and coins at her feet as she came in. In Gruzia the groom would set a white fowl free from the roof of the house and drop rice, wheat and raisins on the bride's head.

In Salonika, another custom was for the groom to buy live fish and put *Fertility* them in a brass bowl; on the eighth day after the wedding the bride jumped three times over this bowl to the blessings of the guests "May you be as fertile as the fish." In Kurdistan the bride held a male infant as the assembled guests called out "May your first be a boy too." In Persia the groom planted three sticks in the courtyard of his house and uprooted them on the sixth day after the wedding and threw them behind him to ward off evil spirits.

Among the mountain Jews of Libya nearly all weddings take place two *Races* days before Sukkot. On the second day of the festival all the grooms participate in foot races symbolic of "and he is a bridegroom coming out of his chamber, and rejoiceth as a strong man to run his course." In Tunisia, on the fifth day after the wedding a competition between bride and groom is arranged in which they each have to dissect a large cooked fish for serving. The groom is always at a disadvantage in that he is given a blunt knife.

The custom of examining the bride's linen after the first night for spots *Test of* of blood as a proof of her virginity is very ancient and is still occasionally *Virginity* practiced in some Oriental communities. The mother of the bride would preserve the sheet to uphold the family honor if later required.

If either the bride or groom become mourners because of a death in the family after the wedding ceremony the seven days of festivities continue and the period of mourning is then observed.

48

6. SPECIAL CEREMONIES

Levirate Marriage and Ḥaliẓah

Levirate marriage is the marriage between a widow whose husband died without offspring and the brother of the deceased (known as levir). When the levir does not marry the *yevamah* (his brother's widow), the ceremony of *ḥaliẓah* takes place whereby the woman becomes released from the levirate tie and becomes free to marry someone else.

The levirate ceremony is only necessary if the deceased has had no chil- *Circumstances* dren whatever, whether from his present wife or former wives, including a child conceived during his lifetime but not born until after his death, even if that child subsequently died. Furthermore, levirate marriage can apply only to brothers of the deceased who were born prior to his death, the levir being the eldest of the surviving brothers. Thus if the birth of the levir precedes his brother's death by one day, the woman must wait until he reaches the age of 13 years and one day, when he becomes legally fit either to marry her or grant her *ḥaliẓah*. The laws of levirate marriage apply only to paternal brothers. If the deceased had several wives then a levirate marriage with any one wife suffices and exempts the others. If however, any one of the wives is prohibited from marrying the levir (e.g., she is his daughter who married her uncle) then all wives are exempt from the obligation. Only a putative marriage can be contracted between a woman awaiting levirate marriage or *ḥaliẓah* and another man. In such a case the man is obliged to give her a divorce, although the offspring are not considered *mamzerim*.

Although in biblical law no ceremony is attached to levirate marriage, *Ceremony* scholars have instituted that the ceremony be just as for all other women, i.e., the declaration with the ring followed by cohabitation.

In modern times the trend has been to prefer *ḥaliẓah* to levirate mar- *Ḥaliẓah* riage. One reason given is because of the enactment that a man can have only one wife thus preventing him who is married from taking his brother's widow as a second. For the sake of uniformity, levirate marriage has been abandoned even in cases where the brother is not married.

49

A *ḥaliẓah* ceremony as depicted in a German engraving, 1734.

The *ḥaliẓah* ceremony is invested with a special solemnity. The normal court consisting of three ordained rabbis is augmented for the occasion by two additional members (who can be laymen). The five members of the court meet at the place where the ceremony is to take place on the previous day, in order to establish the locality. The ceremony takes place the following morning and the woman is enjoined to fast until the ceremony. She and the levir are also instructed, if necessary, to repeat the respective declarations which they have to make in the original Hebrew. Questions are put to ascertain that there are no circumstances which might invalidate the ceremony, e.g., to ascertain that both are majors, in full possession of their mental faculties, that ninety-one days have passed since the death of her husband. Although levirate marriage is forbidden at present, the presiding rabbi nevertheless formally asks the

50

levir which he prefers, to marry his sister-in-law or release her through *ḥaliẓah,* to which he replies confirming the latter alternative. The ceremony proper then commences, the essence of which is that the woman has to draw a special shoe off the foot of her brother-in-law. The *ḥaliẓah* shoe must conform rigidly to specific halakhic regulations. It must be made of leather including the sewing, the loops, and the straps, no metal whatsoever being permitted. It resembles a moccasin, and is fastened primarily with three loops. Since the shoe must be the property of the levir, it is given to him as an unconditional gift. He tries it on his right foot and is asked to walk in it, to see that it fits, even when unlaced; he repeats the procedure after it is tied in the prescribed manner, first by fastening the loops and then winding the straps around it. The laces are then undone.

Until recent times, in Eastern Europe it was the custom for the levir to *The Shoe* lean against an upturned board used for the ritual washing of a corpse, in order to emphasize that his status and rights as a levir are derived from the death of his brother; this rather morbid custom has been abandoned. The levir nowadays leans against a beam or a wall and presses his foot hard on the ground. The woman then makes the following declaration, in Hebrew: "My husband's brother refuses to raise up unto his brother a name in Israel; he will not perform the duty of a husband's brother

Ḥaliẓah shoe from Germany, 19th century.

51

unto me," to which he answers, also in Hebrew, and in one breath, the three words meaning "I do not want to take her." The woman then bends down, places her left hand on the calf of her brother-in-law and with the right hand undoes the laces and loops. She raises his leg, slips off the shoe, and casts it away. She then collects some ordure in her mouth, spits on the floor in front of him and declares in Hebrew: "So shall it be done unto the man that doth not build up his brother's house; and his name shall be called in Israel *bet haluẓ ha-na'al*" ("the house of him that had his shoe loosened"). All those present thrice repeat the last three words. The members of the court then recite the formula "may it be the divine will that the daughters of Israel shall be liable neither to levirate marriage nor *haliẓah*."

In order to avoid the situation in which the levir refused to release his sister-in-law by *haliẓah* or demands some payment for it, it was customary in Germany and England for the prospective levir to sign a document at the time of his brother's marriage committing himself to perform *haliẓah* should the need arise (see page 99). In most communities, however, the practice was considered morbid and was not followed.

Agency
It is conceivable, although not probable, that a proper and legal wedding take place, all in accordance with Jewish law, at which either the groom or the bride is not present. Furthermore, the transaction binding the absentee party may indeed be effected between two men or two women. This situation arises from a legal concept known as agency whereby the lawful acts of someone authorized by, and acting on behalf of, another are as effective as if performed by the principal.

The principal must state his or her wishes clearly, for example, "Go and marry any woman in this city for me," or "accept on my behalf marriage from such and such a man."

The agent must act completely in accordance with the mandate he received; any deviation may lead to an invalidation of his mission. The wedding formula pronounced by the agent differs only slightly from the regular, "Behold you are consecrated unto *so and so* according to the law of Moses and Israel."

Although this method of marriage is effective, the Talmud states that it is a greater *mitzvah* to perform the marriage act oneself rather than by agency.

Conditional Marriage

Marriage on condition, e.g., when a man says to a woman, "Behold, you are consecrated unto me with this (penny) on condition that I later give you one hundred dollars . . . ," is legally binding provided it satisfies four conditions: 1) repetition of the statement is made; the above declaration must end with "and if I don't give you one hundred dollars, you will not be consecrated unto me," 2) the positive is stated before the negative, i.e., "you will be consecrated" prior to "you will not be," 3) the fulfillment of the condition shall not retroactively effect a marriage but will begin the bond from its fulfillment, and 4) the condition is attainable, e.g., a condition such as "that I shall not breathe for one hour," being impossible nullifies the condition.

Because the law of conditions is complicated, and because marriage should provide real security, the practice of marriage by condition has almost completely vanished.

Deaf-Mute, Insane

While according to the Bible a deaf-mute cannot contract a marriage, the rabbis enacted otherwise. In such a case, someone who is familiar with the appropriate sign language attends the ceremony and explains the significance of the act of betrothal. The groom then places the ring on the bride's right hand as usual, the declaration being understood from the preceding sign language. If both groom and bride are deaf-mutes the blessings are not recited by the rabbi since they could not recite them themselves. If one of the parties is not a deaf mute there are opinions that the benedictions should be recited.

53

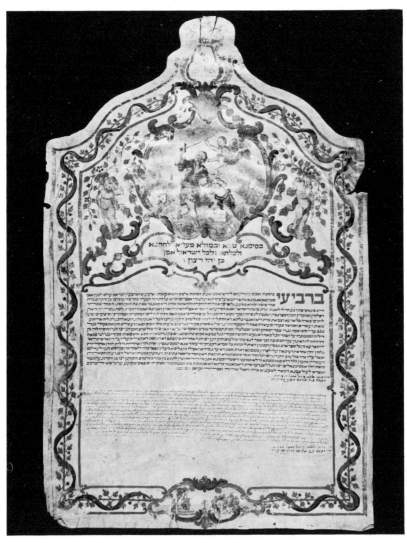

A *ketubbah* from Ancona, 1784. An additional agreement is recorded after the usual *ketubbah* text.

An insane person cannot contract a marriage. If that person has lucid moments a marriage could be contracted during those intervals. If it is unknown whether at the time of marriage the individual was in possession of his faculties or not, the subsistence of the marriage is doubtful but is viewed as if it were valid.

7. SAMARITAN MARRIAGE

The Samaritans refer to the act of engagement as *kiddushin*. It is effected *Engagement* as follows: When a girl is certain of her choice, she urges him to request his parents to ask her parents for her hand. Occasionally, when a young man is in love he may request his parents to approach the girl's parents even without telling her of it. On being asked, the girl's parents reply: "We will call the damsel, and inquire at her mouth." The girl's wish is now tested. If she desires the man though her parents are opposed, she may reply affirmatively, in which case, she appoints a guardian to perform the betrothal on her behalf. The engagement takes place in the girl's home, and even a minor Samaritan priest can sustain the bond and bless it by recital of the *Shema* and similar verses from the Pentateuch. The breaking of the engagement does not require a divorce. Whenever conditions do not permit the continuance of the attachment, the man informs the girl's parents in writing or by word of mouth and he is not liable for damages.

The next step is the betrothal, referred to as *erusin*, which takes place a *Betrothal* short time after the *kiddushin*. Release from *erusin* requires a divorce. The girl is herself not present, but her representative, her father or her uncle, or, in the event of her father not consenting to the betrothal, the guardian, sits opposite the young man. They clasp right hands together as a sign of the bond. The high priest sitting opposite, places his right hand upon their clasped hands and pronounces the betrothal blessings over the bond. The high priest then receives a tied handkerchief containing six silver shekels from the young man and hands them to the girl's representative as a symbol of the bride-price. When the priest finishes

55

A Samaritan betrothal ceremony with the groom and the bride's father (a priest) on either side of the high priest.

reading, "It is not good that the man should be alone; I will make him a helpmeet for him," the fiancé kisses the hand of the priest and the notables. The couple are now regarded as husband and wife.

The Samaritan marriage ceremony is the formal act whose purpose it *Marriage* is to complete the betrothal. Rejoicing on this occasion is greater than at any Samaritan ceremony. The bridegroom's family proclaims a week of rejoicing to begin the Sabbath before the wedding. On this Sabbath the weekly portion of the law is read in the house of the groom's father. When the afternoon service is completed, the groom's relatives walk in procession from house to house and invite guests to take part in the week of rejoicing. At the termination of the Sabbath, the men have a great feast in the house of the groom's father and sing wedding songs. The father of the groom bestows gifts upon the honored guests. On Sunday evening the women arrange their feast in the house of the bride's mother where there is much singing and music. On Monday evening one of the groom's relatives invites the men to a feast prepared in his house, and they again indulge in hymn singing and praise. In the center of the party sit the men, who sing verse by verse the account of Rebekkah's marriage to Isaac, each man taking a turn, with the bridegroom completing the reading.

56

The evening of the third day is called "the red night," the night of the *Red Night* rejoicing of the bride. She is clothed in red garments symbolizing her virginity. The women prepare a splendid feast for her, the high point of which is the dance of the bridegroom's father holding a parcel decorated with flowers containing the garments of the groom. The wedding takes place on the fourth day when the luminaries, symbolized by the bridegroom and bride, were created. During the day the bridegroom takes a piece of parchment to one of the scholars among the priests and asks him to write the marriage contract. He also rewards him for his trouble. In the evening the men assemble in the house of the groom, where they partake of the marriage feast.

Afterward the groom's father invites the high priest to the place of re- *The High* joicing where the marriage is to take place. The high priest, the bride- *Priest* groom, and the guests await the coming of the bride. She is accompanied by her relatives, who both dance and sing the Song of the Red Sea (the song of the prophetess Miriam) to the music of tambourines. On the bride's arrival the priests break out in poetic song and marriage psalms. When the singing is finished, the groom rises, hands the marriage contract to the high priest, and kisses his right hand. The priest reads it slowly, and then details the virtues and rank of the families of the bridegroom and bride and the conditions upon which their marriage is taking place. When the reading ends the contract is handed to the bride's representative, her father, uncle, or guardian, for safekeeping. The groom kisses the hands of the high priest, gives him his fee and receives a wedding gift from him. The groom then turns to the bride, lifts the veil from her head, kisses her, and places a ring upon her finger. Sometimes they strengthen the bond by drinking wine from the same cup. During the following Sabbath prayers, songs signifying the joy of marriage are added to the services in the synagogue. These are sung by the priest except when the groom is of a priestly family, in which case a lay Samaritan sings them. The groom reads the weekly portion of the law. A festive meal is held after the reading of the portion; this concludes the week of marriage.

8. MARITAL OBLIGATIONS

The act of marriage creates certain rights and duties between husband and wife. In performing them, both parties have to conduct themselves according to the following rules, comprising the fundamental principles for the relationship between husband and wife in Jewish law: "Thus the sages laid down that a man shall honor his wife more than his own self and shall love her as he loves himself, and shall constantly seek to benefit her according to his means; that he shall not unduly impose his authority on her and shall speak gently with her; that he shall be neither sad nor unstable. Similarly they laid down that a wife shall honor her husband exceedingly and shall accept his authority and abide by his wishes in all her activities. . . . "

The marital obligations are briefly formulated in the *ketubbah* which is a document written in Aramaic, an ancient vernacular of the Jews, and which is read during the ceremony (see page 36). The actual form of the *ketubbah* dates from the early Middle Ages and basically consists of two parts: 1) The main *ketubbah* and its increment—the amount determined by law as the minimum the wife is entitled to receive from her husband should he divorce her (a sort of alimony) or from his estate should he pre-decease her, and 2) The dowry and its increment—that which the husband renders himself liable to return to his wife as the equivalent of her dowry in either of the above circumstances. Except for the minimum fixed by law there is no need to state the exact amounts involved and that is the usual practice. In some communities, however, an overall aggregate amount is stated.

The Ketubbah Document

In recent years a clause has been added to the *ketubbah* used by Conservative congregations in the United States. In this addition both bride and groom agree that should either so demand the other will appear before a rabbinical court and accept its verdict. This clause was introduced to avoid the situation in which after a civil divorce had been granted one of the parties would refuse to either give or accept a Jewish divorce (see page 76) and thus prevent the other from contracting a further marriage.

Conservative Practice

Ketubbah from London 1835.

Ketubbah from Safed, 1866.

A husband has ten obligations toward his wife and four rights in respect *Force of* of her. These rights and duties both derive from law and not from mere *Law* agreement between the parties: "a man, by marrying a woman, becomes obligated to her in ten matters and acquires rights against her in four matters, even if they have not been committed to writing," i.e., the said rights and duties devolve as a matter of law from the act of marriage, whether or not a *ketubbah* deed is written and "writing them does not add and the absence thereof does not detract."

The first and second obligations of the husband are to provide sus- *Sustenance and* tenance and maintenance. This includes the supply of all necessities *Maintenance* such as food, raiment, lodging, furniture, utensils, etc. The husband must support his wife by the rule that she "goes up with him but does not go down with him," i.e., the wife is entitled to a standard of living which matches that of her husband and to be maintained in accordance with his means and social standing. At the same time, she is not obliged to suffer having her standard of living reduced to one below that which she enjoyed prior to her marriage, at any rate not as compared with the standard of living customary in her paternal home backed by means similar to those available to her husband, even if he should choose a lower standard of living than he can afford.

The third obligation of the husband is cohabitation. The obligation to do *Cohabitation* so is dependent on the husband's physical ability and regard is given to the requirements of his occupation. If the husband is unable to fulfill this duty the wife is entitled to demand a divorce unless there are reasonable prospects, on the strength of medical evidence, that he may be cured of his disability.

The fourth obligation concerns the main *ketubbah*, which the husband *Ketubbah* must pay at the dissolution of the marriage.

The fifth obligation concerns the payment of medical expenses in case of *Medical* the wife's illness. *Expenses*

The sixth obligation is for the husband to provide the money and to per- *Captivity* form any other act required to redeem his wife from captivity.

The seventh obligation is the husband's duty to bear the costs of his wife's *Burial*
burial and all related expenses such as those necessary for erecting a
tombstone.

The eighth and ninth obligations are the support of the widow and of *Support*
the minor daughters from his estate upon his death (see page 68). *after Death*

The last obligation is the inheritance by the sons of the marriage of their *Inheritance*
mother's *ketubbah,* over and above their rightful portion in the estate
of their father. This refers to a condition in the *ketubbah* whereby the
husband agrees that his wife's *ketubbah* and dowry, which he—as by
law he is her only heir—would inherit if she predeceased him, shall,
upon his own death, pass to the sons of the marriage only.

The first right the husband has is to the wife's handiwork. It is the wife's *Handiwork*
duty to do all such household work as is normally performed by women
enjoying a standard of living and social standing similar to that of the
spouse; all in accordance with local custom. The wife need not do the
kind of work that was not customarily done by the women in her family
circle prior to her marriage, although according to the husband's standard women used to do it, while at the same time she is entitled to benefit
from the fact that her husband enjoys a higher standard of living than
that to which she was accustomed prior to the marriage. Within the framework of this responsibility, the wife is not liable for damage caused by
her in the home—e.g., in respect of broken utensils—whether or not
occasioned in the course of fulfillment of her duties.

The second right to the husband entitles him to the finds or chance gains *Found*
of his wife. Thus, if she finds lost property, it belongs to him. *Property*

The third right of the husband entitles him to the usufruct of some of *Nikhsei*
the wife's property. The property the wife brings into marriage is divided *Zon Barzel*
into three categories. Firstly, *nikhsei zon barzel* ("the property of iron
sheep"), which is that part of the wife's property given over to the husband's ownership but under his responsibility, i.e., subject to his undertaking to restore to her the value thereof as fixed in the *ketubbah* upon

62

dissolution of the marriage. If at the time of the recovery the property is still in existence, the wife is entitled to demand the property in specie, and neither the husband nor the heirs can compel her to accept money instead.

The second type of property is *nikhsei melog*—property of which the principal remains in the wife's ownership but the fruits thereof are taken by the husband. Thus, any loss or gain on the principal belong to the wife and upon dissolution of the marriage the property returns to the wife as it stands, in specie. *Nikhsei Melog*

The last category of property is that to which the husband has no rights whatsoever, neither to the principal nor to the fruits. This includes property acquired by her after the marriage by way of gift, the donor having expressly stipulated that it be used for a specific purpose, or property given to her as a gift by her husband.

The husband in all three cases has no rights to the principal, i.e., with *nikhsei zon barzel* because the woman retains the right to reclaim the property in specie after dissolution of the marriage and in the other two categories by their nature in law. However, all the fruits of the wife's property, i.e., all benefits derived from her property in a manner leaving intact the principal and its continued capacity to provide benefits—such as natural or legal fruits, e.g., rental, the right to occupation or stock dividends—belong to the husband. *Rights to Principal*

The last right of the husband concerns inheritance, i.e., he is sole heir of his wife—to the absolute exclusion of everyone, including her children. *Inheritance*

Just as the husband has a duty to cohabit with his wife, the woman may not persistently refuse cohabitation. The woman who does so refuse is called a *moredet* and if she persists for a minimum period of twelve months she may be liable to be divorced without receiving the benefit of her *ketubbah*. During this period the husband is not responsible for her maintainance. *Cohabitation*

9. FAMILY PURITY

Family purity (*taharat ha-mishpahah*) is the term popularly given to the laws of *niddah* (menstruant woman), which involve a married couple's abstinence from sexual relations during the period of menstruation until the wife's immersion in the *mikveh* (ritual bath). These regulations are considered by Orthodox Jews to be basic to the Jewish way of life, and Rabbi Akiva went so far as to declare the child conceived while the mother was a *niddah*, a *mamzer*. Although his viewpoint is not accepted as the *halakhah*, it nevertheless indicates the importance of these laws. In more modern times, many psychological, medical, and physiological reasons have been given for the observance of this precept all of which stress the benefits that are gained by the couple practicing abstinence during part of each month. Societies have been organized in many communities for the purpose of instructing people in the family laws and supervising the daily functioning of the ritual bath.

The laws relating to the menstruous woman comprise some of the most *Place in* fundamental principles of the halakhic system. They are among the most *Halakhah* difficult and intricate in the entire range of *halakhah*, and their historical development through the centuries is extremely complicated. To decide a law relating to a menstruous woman demands, besides a profound knowledge of the *halakhah*, experience in various medical matters, and at times also the capacity to assume the grave responsibility of preventing a woman from pursuing a normal married life and of—at times—separating her forever from her husband.

In the Bible the laws of the *niddah* are listed among the general laws of *Biblical* ritual impurity having to do with the priesthood and the Sanctuary *Law* (later, the Temple). This aspect is no longer relevant after the destruction of the Temple. However the biblical law of *niddah* has another dimension, i.e., that sexual intercourse is prohibited while the woman is in a state of being a *niddah*. The basic biblical law is as follows: a woman who discerns blood within and up to a period of seven days is "impure" for those seven days from the time the blood first appears. On the eighth day—if she sees no further blood—she becomes "pure" after immersion in the ritual bath. If she, however, sees blood for more than seven days, she becomes a *zavah* and must wait until the cessation of the discharge and an additional seven "clean" days thereafter. Once again immersion in the ritual bath is presumed to be a part of the purification ceremony.

The biblical passage which is, however, by no means clear was interpreted in the Talmud and has had additions made to it in later times. These additions do not change the original law but enlarge its scope. Other aspects of *niddah* have also been the subject of constant discussion, such as, which colored discharges are to be considered as blood, or what amount is necessary to constitute a discharge. *Development*

In brief, the *halakhah* as at present codified is that sexual intercourse (and any other intimacies which may lead to it) is forbidden from the time the woman expects her menses until seven "clean" days (i.e., days on which no blood whatsoever is seen) have elapsed. A minimum of five days is fixed for the menses themselves. Thus the minimum period of separation is twelve days. In the evening of the seventh day the woman immerses herself in a *mikveh* and normal marital relations are resumed until the next menses are expected. Any bleeding is considered as menstrual and requires a waiting period of seven "clean" days. *Present Day*

A *mikveh* is a ritual bathhouse that must meet many specifications. The water of the *mikveh* must be natural, i.e., not drawn in a vessel or receptacle and deposited in the *mikveh*, but rather gathered into the *mikveh* by natural means. A prefabricated building will fall into the category of a vessel placed in the ground and thereby invalidate the water therein. Other requirements place the minimum amount of water as forty se'ah (according to various calculations between 250–1,000 liters) and the water may not be discolored by any admixtures. Such requirements obviously create great difficulties particularly in places with a low rainfall. Many ingenious methods have been devised to construct *mikva'ot* according to the *halakhah*. The most common is to collect the required amount of "natural" water in a storage cistern which is connected to the actual bath *Mikveh* by an aperture in the common wall. The bath is filled and emptied at will with ordinary tap-water. When it is filled it becomes connected to the natural water in the cistern through the aperture and thus itself becomes a valid *mikveh*.

Cleansing oneself in an ordinary bath or shower cannot replace the necessity of immersion in the *mikveh*. On the other hand, immersion in the *mikveh* must be preceded by careful cleansing of the body. The purpose of immersion is therefore not physical, but spiritual, cleanliness. Maimonides wrote, "It is plain that the laws about immersion as a means of freeing oneself from uncleanness are decrees laid down by Scripture and not matters about which human understanding is capable of forming a judgement; for behold, they are included among the divine statutes. Now 'uncleanness' is not mud or filth which water can remove, but is a matter of Scriptural decree and dependent on the intention of the heart. Therefore, the sages have said, 'If a man immerses himself, but without special intention, it is as though he has not immersed himself at all.'

"Nevertheless we may find some indication (for the moral basis) of this: *Spirituality* Just as one who sets his heart on becoming clean becomes clean as soon as he has immersed himself, although nothing new has befallen his body, so, too, one who sets his heart on cleansing himself from the uncleanness that beset men's souls—namely, wrongful thoughts and false convictions—becomes clean as soon as he consents in his heart to shun those counsels and brings his soul into the waters of pure reason. Behold, Scriptures say, 'And I will sprinkle clean water upon you and ye shall be clean; from all your uncleannesses and from all your idols will I cleanse you.'"

In modern times there has been a continuing decrease in the observance *Modern* of the laws of family purity particularly among Jews in Western coun- *Attitudes* tries; the Reform movement does not consider these laws—together with many other laws of a ritual nature—to be valid in the modern world. However, of late an effort is being made in more traditional circles to reeducate for the observance of these laws and to find spiritual significance in them relevant to modern man. One eminent Orthodox scholar has called these laws the way to make one's marriage a perpetual honeymoon and sees them as means of revitalising the institution of marriage.

10. TERMINATION OF MARRIAGE

Marriage can be terminated in Jewish law in only one of two ways, divorce or death of one of the parties. There are cases recorded in the Talmud of the retroactive annulment of marriage; however, this has not been practiced for several centuries (see page 78).

Widowhood

Upon the death of a spouse, varying periods of time are observed before *The Waiting* the surviving spouse may enter a new marriage. A widower may remar- *Period* ry after the three pilgrim festivals (Passover, Shavuot, and Sukkot) have passed. If he has small children in need of a mother's care, or if he has not as yet satisfied the requirements of the procreational commandment, i.e., being the father of one male and one female child, the restrictions are relaxed and marriage may take place after observance of one month of mourning. A widow may not remarry for three months; this rule is in order to avoid any doubt as to the paternity of a child to which she may subsequently give birth.

The death of a spouse is established by the testimony of witnesses; where- *Evidence* as in most other cases where evidence is required, two witnesses are needed, in this case the testimony of one witness, who may even be a woman, is sufficient to establish the new status for the remaining spouse.

A husband inherits his wife's estate and is later obliged to pay the worth *Inheritance* of her *ketubbah* to her children upon his death. This obligation precedes *of the* the children's right to inheritance; thus, his children from another wife *Ketubbah* have no claim to the contents of this *ketubbah*.

67

Numerous legal enactments provide the widow with the necessary sup- port required by her status. Although the widow does not inherit her hus- band's estate, she is entitled to payment of her *ketubbah* from his heirs, and until such time as she receives it she is entitled to maintenance from his property. Furthermore, she cannot be forced to accept payment of her *ketubbah*, but may choose to receive maintenance for as long a period as she desires. However, if she remarries, this choice will not be avail- able to her and she must accept the payment of the *ketubbah* from her children.

Although in Jewish law a daughter does not inherit her father if there are sons (or descendants of sons), the *ketubbah* pledges the groom's estate for support of his minor daughters upon his death, and in the ab- sence of such a clause, this support may be assumed by construing the omission as an error. Many pages of Jewish law deal with this problem and ultimately, the right to support of female orphans came to over- shadow the claims of all other heirs, and, if need be, the entire estate was used for this purpose. This provision aided the widow in providing for the female children and placed responsibility directly on the bene- factors of the estate. In the case of impoverished orphan children whose father left little or no property, where neither the estate nor the widow can provide support, the Talmud holds the community responsible for their support, for marrying them off, and for providing them with the means to live economically independent lives. Communal funds were to be used to rent and furnish a house for a young man and to outfit a girl with clothing and a minimum dowry.

Divorce

In ancient Israel a man could divorce his wife at will and send her away: "the woman goes out whether she pleases or not, but the husband sends her out only if it so pleases him." The Bible does not detail the method or ceremony of divorce: "When a man taketh a wife, and marrieth her, then it cometh to pass, if she find no favour in his eyes, because he hath found some unseemly thing in her, that he writeth her a bill of divorce- ment, and giveth it in her hand, and sendeth her out of his house. And she departeth out of his house, and goeth and becometh another man's wife." The specific text of the bill, the ceremony of the giving of the bill and any financial conditions between parties are not mentioned and can only be assumed.

Only two situations are recorded in the Bible, in which a man is prohibited from divorcing his wife: 1) when he has falsely accused her of prenuptial intercourse, and 2) when the marriage is a result of his having raped her. Contrary to expectations, the Bible does not relate any instances of divorce being given lightly. Abraham was hesitant in sending away his concubine, Paltiel wept when he had to give up Michal, and Ezra encountered significant opposition when he called on the men to give up their foreign wives.

The ideal of marriage was that of a permanent union: "Therefore shall a man leave his father and his mother, and shall cleave unto his wife, and they shall be one flesh." Divorce, however, did remain necessary. It was probably resorted to most often in the event of the barrenness of the marital union.

The divorced woman's lot was an unpleasant one. Generally she returned *Children* to her father's home, leaving her children with her former husband. Special arrangements were probably made for suckling infants; in later law, boys, at least, had to be returned to their father's house by the age of six. The divorcée was free to marry, but was prohibited to a priest. Moral anguish speaks out of Malachi's denunciation of the frequency of divorce in Judea in the fifth century B.C.E. At about the same time, the Jewish military colony in Elephantine seems to have adopted practices *Elephantine* from their Egyptian neighbors which strengthened the woman's position *Practice* in her marriage. In the extant marriage documents of that group each spouse was given the power to dissolve the marriage. The husband, furthermore, had to return his wife's dowry regardless of who had initiated the divorce, and he had to give her all of her possessions before she was required to depart from his house. These Elephantine provisions were never accepted into Jewish law although some similarities may seem to exist.

69

The Talmud's attitude toward divorce is similar to that of the Bible; *In the* the talmudic sages extend the phrase "because he hath found some *Talmud* unseemly thing in her to include any kind of obnoxious behavior or what-soever brings him to hate her. Although it was and still is easy for a man to divorce his wife, laws of writing and delivery of the *get* (bill of divorce-ment) were enacted in order to slow down the process so that a man would not act rashly, and indeed one reason given in the Talmud for the institution of the *ketubbah* is "that the daughters of Israel should not be easy in the eyes of their husbands to divorce." However, one important *Mutual* innovation did take place by a rabbinical enactment, prohibiting a man *Consent* from divorcing his wife against her will. Jewish divorce, as it is practiced today is very much the same as the Talmudic institution.

A Jewish divorce differs from divorce in most other systems in that it is an *The Court* act of the parties to the marriage, not an act of the court. In Jewish law, the court's function is to decide whether or not one of the parties can be obliged to give or receive a divorce if no mutual agreement between them exists and to supervise the writing and handing over of the document; however, a court decree that a divorce is necessary does not change the status of the marriage. Only the delivery of a proper *get* by the husband to the wife can change that status. Furthermore, while in secular divorce law, a court is required to establish a reason for the breakup of marriage and in some instances, only adultery is adequate grounds for divorce, in Jewish law a decision by the couple to terminate their marriage is suffi-cient reason for its dissolution. The courts must see to it that the divorce is done properly but they can in no way effect the change of status. In addition, because a divorce requires mutual consent, if at any time prior to the giving of the *get*, either the husband or wife reconsider their decision, all the marital obligations are in effect, and a court order for divorce cannot eliminate these obligations.

Whereas, in general, divorce needs the consent of the parties, under cer-tain circumstances either party may demand a divorce. In such a case the court may assist in obtaining an agreement from the second party by imposing a fine or by imprisonment.

בחמישי בשבת בשני ימים לירח שבט שנת חמשת אלפים ושבע מאות ושמנה עשרה לבריאת עולם

למנין שאנו מנין כאן ביאהאנעסבורג מתא דיתבא על מי מעינות במדינת

טראנסוואאל דרום אפריקא אנא מאיר בן אהרן הכהן דמתקרי ארא העומד היום

ביאהאנעסבורג מתא דיתבא על מי מעינות במדינת טראנסוואאל דרום אפריקא

צביתי ברעות נפשי בדלא אניסנא ושבקית ופטרית ותרוכית יתיכי

ליכי אנת אנתתי צפורה המכונה ציפי בת שמעון הכהן דהוית אנתתי

מן קדמת דנא וכדן פטרית ושבקית ותרוכית יתיכי ליכי

די תיהויין רשאה ושלטאה בנפשיכי למהך להתנסבא

לכל גבר די תיצביין ואנש לא ימחא בידיכי

מן יומא דנן ולעלם והרי את מותרת לכל אדם

ודן די יהוי ליכי מנאי ספר תרוכין ואגרת שבוקין וגט פטורין

כד ת משה ה וישר א

יוסף בן אברהם עד

יעקב צבי בן שרגא עד

Either the existence of physical defects in one's spouse or a claim of *Grounds for* "misconduct" are sufficient grounds for demanding a divorce. In this *Divorce* context "physical defects" refers to the inability of a spouse to cohabit because of either a defect in the sexual organ or because of some other defect that arouses feelings of revulsion in the spouse which prevents cohabitation. A spouse is similarly entitled to demand a divorce by "physical defect" if the marriage remains childless for a minimum period of ten years. However, the court will not entertain any claim of defect if a spouse has had prior knowledge that the defect existed or if upon acquiring such knowledge the couple continue to live together. If, on the other hand, it can be shown that the delay can be accounted for and no waiver of right was intended the court will aid in obtaining the divorce. Any defect, no matter how serious, if it does not preclude the possibility of cohabitation will not suffice to demand a divorce.

A claim of "misconduct" includes a spouse's unjustified refusal to co- *Misconduct* habit or carry out the marital obligations. "Misconduct" may also be claimed if either party is habitually assaulted or insulted or if either is forced to transgress Jewish law by the other. The court will direct the parties to attempt to live together for an additional period in order to ascertain whether a divorce is the only answer, unless it is satisfied that no purpose will be served by such a delay.

In addition to these cases, the court will compel a divorce upon the re- *Prohibited* quest of either party to a prohibited but valid marriage (see page 86), *Marriage* regardless of whether or not they had knowledge of the prohibition, as a matter of law or fact, and regardless of their continued cohabitation after becoming aware of the prohibition.

To be valid, a *get* must be given by the husband of his free will and is *Compulsion* therefore invalid if given while he is of unsound mind, or under duress. However, if the court compels him to give a *get*—as in the above cases— then the *get* will not be considered to have been given under duress, since he has no right to refuse to give it. To insure that the divorce is given of his free will, it is customary for the husband to annul all declarations in which he purported to have been compelled to give a *get*.

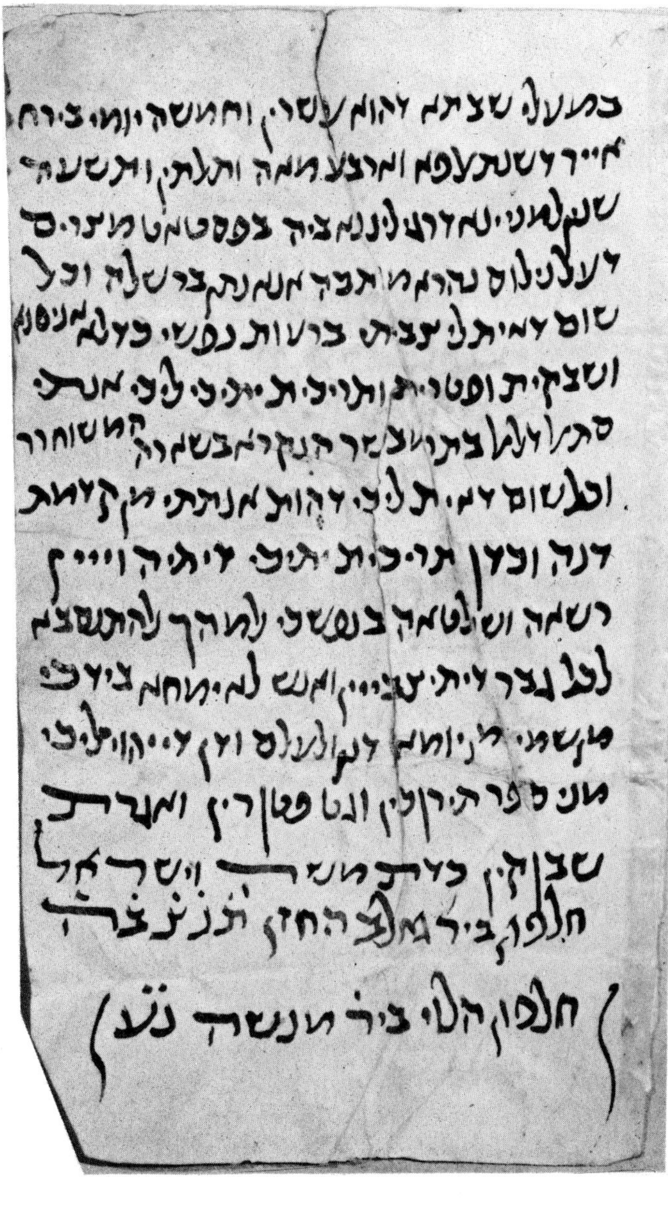

An 11/12th century divorce document from Fostat (old Cairo).

Divorce is carried into effect by the *get* being written, signed, and delivered by the husband to the wife. It is written by a scribe upon the husband's instruction to write "for him, for her, and for the purpose of divorce." The materials used in the writing must belong to the husband and the scribe formally presents them as an outright gift to the husband before the writing commences. The strictest care must be taken in the formula of the *get*, most of it in Aramaic, and the text is, with minor differences, according to the wording given in the Talmud (see page 100). To obviate errors, it is still the practice to write the *get* in Aramaic, although a *get* in any language would be valid. Care must be taken to write the correct date on which the *get* is written, signed, and delivered, otherwise it can be invalidated. Sexual relations between the husband and wife are prohibited from the time of the writing of the *get*. Two witnesses must see the writing of the *get* and two witnesses must be present at its delivery. (Usually one pair of witnesses perform both functions.) After the wife receives the *get* she gives it to the court, who present her with a document stating that she has been divorced according to law. The court then tears the *get* in order to avoid any later suspicion that it was not absolutely legal and files it away in its torn state. The rules pertaining to the writing, signing, and delivery of a *get* are very formal and exact in order to avoid mistakes and they must therefore be stringently observed. As a result it was laid down that "a person who is not expert with the laws of divorce . . . should not deal with them."

Although divorce in Jewish law is the personal act of the husband and wife, their presence in person is not a necessary requirement for its execution. Delivery and receipt of the *get* may be done by agents representing the various parties. Appointment of an agent is done before the court by way of power of attorney. An agent appointed by the husband to deliver the *get* is called "the agent of delivery" and the agent representing the wife to receive the *get*, "agent of receipt." A woman may also appoint an "agent of delivery" who receives the *get* from the husband or his agent for the purpose of delivering it to her. Thus, whereas in the case of her appointing an "agent of receipt" the divorce is valid from the very moment that that agent receives the *get,* in the case of an "agent of delivery" the validity takes hold only from the time the *get* is personally delivered to her. The use of an agent in divorce is of practical importance in cases where husband and wife live in different countries and want to avoid the expense of travel, or when they prefer not to confront each other during the actual divorce ceremony.

A *get* may be written and delivered conditionally, that is so as not to take effect except on fulfillment of a stipulated condition, e.g., if the husband should fail to return to his wife within a specified period or that no word from or concerning him shall be forthcoming until then. The condition must not contradict the basic nature of divorce, i.e., the absolute severance of the marriage relationship. To have validity it is necessary that all the complicated laws pertaining to conditional acts be observed (see page 53). Because of the doubts and complications that may arise, it is general practice not to allow conditional divorces except in exceptional cases, e.g., in times of persecution or war when there is a separation between husband and wife and there is a danger of her becoming an *agunah* (see page 76). In such cases the practice is sometimes adopted of granting a *get* on condition, e.g., if the husband should fail to return from the wars by a certain date then the *get* shall be deemed to be effective and the woman may remarry freely. This type of divorce may also be used by a man on his deathbed who has no children. By virtue of a conditional divorce, the wife upon his death will not be required to undergo *ḥaliẓah* but may remarry as a divorcée. *Conditional Get*

A *kohen* (priest) is prohibited from marrying a divorcée; it follows that he may not remarry even his own former wife. Therefore, a special divorce document was instituted for *kohanim* which involved a greater amount of preparation and thus gave the *kohen* more time to reconsider his action. This document, known as a "knotted" *get,* is not in use today. *Kohen*

In Jewish law, divorce frees the parties to remarry as they please save as prohibited by law. The woman is entitled to a return of her property and for payment of her *ketubbah* except when she forfeits it, for example, *Results of Divorce*

if the divorce is because of her adultery, etc. Upon divorce, the husband is no longer required to maintain his wife; however, it is considered to be an act of charity—and thus a *mitzvah*—if he does so.

Jewish divorce, although burdened by many laws, is executed easily. The overabundance of intricate details, instituted with the passage of time, are intended to slow down the process and are in keeping with the Jewish attitude that divorce should only be employed if all else fails. The fact that God is portrayed as grand matchmaker prompted the reaction that "when a man divorced his wife, even the altar sheds tears."

The Reform movement has discarded the Jewish laws of divorce and its *Reform* rabbis will perform a marriage ceremony on the strength of a civil *Practice* divorce. Some Reform rabbis issue a document to the parties of a civil divorce, certifying that they, the rabbis, consider the parties to be properly divorced.

This practice is the main halakhic basis for the vehement opposition of many Orthodox authorities to the Reform movement since, in the eyes of the former, all children born of such marriages, where the wife had been previously married but had not received a *get* from her first husband, will be *mamzerim* and forbidden in marriage to other Jews. This would lead, in their opinion, to a schism in the Jewish people.

Other Orthodox authorities have tried to solve the problem by suggesting that if the first marriage was performed by a Reform rabbi in accordance with Reform practice, the absence of a *get* would not result in the children of the second marriage being *mamzerim* because the original marriage ceremony is not valid. This, however, is a minority opinion, not accepted by the majority of halakhic authorities.

Agunah
An *agunah* is a married woman who is separated from her husband and yet cannot remarry, either because she cannot obtain a divorce from him, or because it is unknown whether he is still alive. The term is also applied to a widow of a childless man who is awaiting *halizah* but it is unknown whether or not the levir is alive.

The *halakhah* prescribes that a marriage can only be dissolved by divorce or the death of either spouse. According to Jewish law, divorce is effected by the parties themselves. Hence, the absence of the husband or his willful refusal to deliver the *get* preclude any possibility of a divorce. Similarly the mere disappearance of the husband, where there is no proof of his death, is not sufficient for a declaration by the court to the effect that a wife is a widow and her marriage thus terminated. In most cases, the question is whether or not the husband is still alive, but the problem can also arise, for example, if the husband suffers from chronic mental illness making him legally incapable of giving a *get* or simply if he willfully refuses to do so.

Rabbinic scholars have permitted many relaxations in the general laws of evidence in order to relieve the hardships suffered by the *agunah*. On the other hand, great care was always taken to avoid the risk that permission may inadvertently be given for a married woman to contract a second marriage that would be adulterous and result in any children from such a second marriage being *mamzerim*. Achieving both these ends, i.e., to enable the *agunah* to remarry while ensuring that an adulterous union does not result, is the object of intensive discussion in the laws of the *agunah*. *Relaxation of Law*

In view of the unhappy straits in which an *agunah* is likely to find herself, ways were sought already in early times of taking precautions against such an eventuality. Thus it was customary for anyone "going to wars of the House of David, to write a bill of divorce for his wife." This *get* was a conditional one, i.e., becoming effective only should the husband not return from war by a specified date, whereupon the wife would become a divorcee and be entitled to marry another man without having to undergo a levirate marriage or *ḥaliẓah*. In certain countries this practice is adopted even in present times by those going to war, but complications may ensue since the rules and the consequences of a *get* of this nature are beset with halakhic problems, particularly when the husband is a *kohen*, since his wife will be a divorcée if he fails to return by the specified date, and by law he may not thereafter remarry her. One of the solu- *Possible Solutions*

tions suggested was for the husband to grant his wife an unconditional divorce, save that each promises to remarry the other upon the husband's return from war. This, however, would not avail a *kohen* for the reasons mentioned. Furthermore, in the event of the wife's refusal to keep her promise upon her husband's return, the question may arise whether on the strength of the *get* she is free to marry another man, because of the reasonable possibility that the husband intended that the *get* be conditional, i.e., to be of effect only in the event of his failure to return from the war. On this question there is a wide difference of opinion on the part of the authorities without any unanimity being reached. Another solution proposed has been the stipulation of a condition at the time of the marriage to the effect that in certain circumstances the marriage should be considered retroactively void, for instance if the husband should fail, without his wife's permission, to return to her after a long absence of specified duration and should refuse, despite her demand, to grant her a *get;* or if he should die childless, leaving a brother who refuses to fulfill the obligations of a levir, etc. This approach also presents formidable halakhic difficulties and was not generally accepted by the majority of the authorities. A wife who is on bad terms with her husband and can prove the likelihood of her becoming an *agunah,* may possibly obtain an injunction from the court restraining her husband from traveling abroad without granting her a conditional *get,* as mentioned above.

Another method of avoiding the disability of an *agunah* is by the enactment of a *takkanah* by halakhic scholars to the effect that the *kiddushin* would be deemed annulled retroactively upon the fulfillment or nonfulfillment of certain specified conditions, such as the husband being missing or his willful refusal to grant a *get.* But this *takkanah,* based on the rule that "a man takes a woman under the conditions laid down by the rabbis . . . and the rabbis may annul his marriage" has rarely been employed since the 14thcentury. In recent times, particularly in the light of the situation following the Holocaust, it has been suggested that halakhic scholars should adopt one or another of these procedures in order to solve certain problems relating to *agunah.*

78

Reform rabbis will generally accept a declaration of the civil court to the *Reform* effect that the husband is to be presumed dead as enough evidence to permit the *agunah* to remarry.

Finding a way for permitting an *agunah* to remarry is deemed a great *Mitzvah* *mitzvah*. Indeed an onerous application of the law, without justification, and in cases where there is no suspicion of deception, is regarded not only as a failure to perform a *mitzvah*, but even as a transgression. However, in view of the danger of legalizing a possibly adulterous union, it is customary for an *agunah* to be permitted to remarry only after consultation with, and consent having been obtained from other leading scholars.

11. PROHIBITED MARRIAGES

Although marriages are predestined, we are told, somewhat paradoxically, to choose a wife carefully. "A woman of valour who can find? . . . Her children rise up, and call her blessed; Her husband also, and he praiseth her: 'Many daughters have done valiantly, but thou excellest them all.' Grace is deceitful, and beauty is vain; But a woman that feareth the Lord, she shall be praised."

A criterion, which was given great significance—it is still important even *Family* in modern times—was to examine the future bride's family. A young man, the Mishnah records, was instructed, "Lift up thine eyes and see what thou art choosing for thyself. Set not thine eyes on beauty; set thine eyes on family."

Until the destruction of the Second Temple in 70 C.E., a complete geneal- *Genealogy* ogical table of priests was carefully preserved, because among the priestly families a pure and unsullied genealogy was rigidly insisted upon. In addition, what was obligatory and mandatory for priestly families was regarded as desirable for non-priestly families.

A ceremony known as *kezazah* (which has since talmudic times fallen *Kezazah* into disuse) shows the importance of genealogy. The Talmud gives the following description of the ceremony. "How is the *kezazah* performed? If one of the brothers married a woman unsuitable for him, members of the family come and bring a barrel filled with fruit and break it in the town square, saying, 'O brethren of the House of Israel, give ear, our brother, so-and-so, has married an unsuitable woman and we are afraid lest his seed mingle with our seed. Come and take yourselves a sign for generations (which are to come), that his seed mingle not with our seed.'"

However, aside from what is only considered as good advice in modern times, biblical and rabbinic law clearly define those unions that are prohibited. The forbidden unions are prohibited whether with or without marriage. Some of them are considered so grievous that even should an otherwise valid wedding ceremony be celebrated, the state of marriage is not created and the relationship between the parties is exactly as though no ceremony had taken place. Other unions are forbidden, but if a valid ceremony is performed the marriage is binding, and the parties will be obliged to divorce.

Judaism absolutely forbids incest. The general biblical prohibition against *Incest* incest with one's "near of kin" has been held to be limited to the following degrees of consanguinity: mother, stepmother, sister and half-sister, granddaughter, father's and mother's sister, father's brother's wife, daughter-in-law, brother's wife (except when levirate marriage is required), stepdaughter and stepgranddaughter, wife's sister during the former's lifetime, and mother-in-law. A list of another twenty degrees of consanguinity was later drawn up by the sages, however, by way of analogy— albeit not to create additional criminal offenses, but as additional prohibitions of intercourse and impediments to marriage (see chart, page 82–83).

Sodomy, homosexuality and bestiality are all capital offenses in biblical law. Lesbianism is not mentioned in the Bible but talmudic law prohibits it and it is punished by flogging.

While the extra-marital intercourse of a married man is not *per se* a *Adultery* crime in biblical or later Jewish law, that of the married woman (where she had been previously warned) is a capital offense. When it can be proved (or presumed in the case of a betrothed woman before *nissu'in*) that the adultery was committed against her will, only the paramour is held liable (see page 84). Where no previous warning was administered and there was mutual consent, the woman is subsequently prohibited to both men, i.e., her husband and the paramour, forever. Her husband is required to divorce her.

Together, adultery and incest make up one of the three cardinal offenses *Cardinal* which a man may not commit even in order to save himself from certain *Offenses* death, or in order to save another person's life; nor are medical reasons considered to be justification.

A child born of an incestuous or adulterous relationship, the act having *Mamzer* been committed with or without the will of the parties, is a *mamzer*.

Prostitution, both of males and females, which in the Bible denoted in- *Prostitution* discriminate sexual intercourse for payment or as part of a pagan cult, acquired a wider meaning in rabbinic literature. The term "intercourse of prostitution" was applied not only to those forbidden relations in a strict legal sense but also to any promiscuous intercourse outside the framework of marriage, and even to a marriage not celebrated in accordance with Jewish law. Therefore, every sexual act between a man and a woman outside marriage was considered as coming within the definition of prostitution and as such was punishable by flogging. Some scholars limit this law to apply to the woman who is ready to prostitute herself to every man, and consequently make exception in the case of a woman who gives herself solely to one man even without the benefit of marriage.

It is an offense to have intercourse with a woman, including one's wife, *Menstruous* when she is a *niddah* (i.e., during her period of menstruation and sub- *Woman* sequent purification). Indeed, this law adds a dimension to the regimen of chastity, since it includes even an unmarried woman, who presumably is always in a state of *niddah*, not having ritually immersed herself (see page 64).

81

INCESTUOUS

Grandmother; Grandfather's Wife; **Wife's Grandmother**[1]; Great-Aunt[2]

Mother; Step-mother; Wife's Mother[1]; Wife's Stepmother[3]; **Father's Sister; Mother's Sister; Father's Brother's Wife**[4]; Mother's Brother's Wife

Sister; Half-Sister; Brother's Wife[5]; **Wife's Sister**[6]

Daughter; Step-Daughter; Daughter-in-Law[7]

Granddaughter; Wife's Granddaughter; Grandson's Wife

Great-Granddaughter; Wife's Great-Granddaughter

---

1. After wife's death, prohibited but valid according to some scholars.
2. Only applies to a sister or sister-in-law of a mother's mother or a father's father: according to some scholars these cases are permitted.
3. Not prohibited at all according to some scholars.
4. If father and brother are not of the same father the marriage is prohibited but valid.
5. Except through levirate marriage.
6. After wife's death marriage is permitted.
7. Wife's daughter-in-law is permitted.

Bold typeface indicates that the prohibition is pentateuchal and the marriage is void. Ordinary typeface indicates that the prohibition is rabbinical and that the marriage is valid.

RELATIONSHIPS

Grandfather; **Grandmother's Husband**; Husband's Grandfather

Father; **Step-Father**; **Father-in-Law**

Brother; **Half-Brother**; **Sister's Husband**[1]; Husband's Brother[2]

Son; **Step-Son**; **Son-in-Law**[3]; Husband's Son-in-Law[4]; **Brother's Son**;

 Sister's Son; **Husband's Brother's Son**[5]; Husband's Sister's Son

Grandson; Husband's Grandson; **Granddaughter's Husband**[6]; Great-Nephew[7]

Great-Grandson; Husband's Daughter's Son's Son[4]; Great-Granddaughter's
 Husband

---

1. During sister's lifetime.
2. Except through levirate marriage.
3. According to some scholars after daughter's death marriage is prohibited but valid.
4. According to some scholars this is not prohibited.
5. Prohibited but valid if husband and brother are not of the same father.
6. According to some scholars after granddaughter's death marriage is prohibited but valid.
7. Only applies to her own or her husband's brother's son's son and sister's daughter's son; according to some scholars these cases are permitted.

Bold typeface indicates that the prohibition is penteuchal and the marriage is void. Ordinary typeface indicates that the prohibition is rabbinical and that the marriage is valid.

83

Rape as such is not a criminal offense in Jewish law. The legal conse- *Rape*
quences of such an act vary with the age of the woman. If she is younger
than twelve years and six months, but older than three, the rapist must
pay the father of the girl fifty *shekels* of silver, as well as compensation
for the pain and shame the girl suffered and the damage caused to her
"marital" value, and then marry her, unless she (or her father) is adverse
to doing so, or unless marriage between them is prohibited by biblical
or rabbinic law. In the case where marriage is carried out, the rapist can
never divorce her (except at her request) and the marriage can only be
terminated by death.

If the girl is older than twelve years and six months the rapist is liable
to compensate only for pain, suffering, shame and blemish. The option
of the woman to force marriage upon him does not apply in this case.

If the sexual relationship takes place with the consent of the female, *Seduction*
the following distinctions are made: if she is older than twelve years
and six months, she is not entitled to any compensation, financial or
otherwise; if she is younger than twelve years, her consent is meaning-
less, and the seducer is considered a rapist and punished accordingly;
if she is between twelve and twelve and six months (*na'arah*) she loses her
claim to compensation for pain and cannot force the seducer to marry
her; she is, however, entitled to payment of the fifty shekel fine and compensation for shame and damage by the seducer.

A married woman who has been raped does not become prohibited to
her husband unless he is a *kohen*, in which case he must divorce her.

It is an offense, punishable by flogging, for a Jew to have intercourse with *Gentile*
a non-Jew. The children of such a relationship follow the female, i.e., if
the female partner were Jewish the child is then a legitimate Jew.

It is similarly an offense, punishable by flogging, to castrate a man by *Castration*
causing injury to his sexual organs. It is also an offense to sterilize a *and*
woman, but it is not punishable as with the man. In some cases pressing *Sterilization*
medical considerations justify setting aside the objections to castration or other forms of deliberate sterilization.

The only sexual offense short of intercourse is "approaching" any per- *"Approaching"* son with whom intercourse is prohibited under penalty of death. Embrac- ing and kissing such persons, and any other precoital activities, are offenses punishable by flogging. But it is no offense to embrace or kiss one's mother, daughter, sister or aunt, or such other relatives who do not normally arouse the sexual urge.

There are several prohibited acts which do not amount to punishable *Minor* offenses, but which may render the perpetrator liable to flogging by way *Offenses* of admonition and rebuke: e.g., indecent gestures or suggestions to wom- en with whom intercourse is prohibited; sexual intercourse with one's wife in public; being secluded with a woman with whom intercourse is prohibited—other than one's mother, daughter or (menstruous) wife, and also except a woman married to another man (because, in the latter case, the flogging might damage her reputation).

Marriages, Prohibited and Void

This category includes: 1) marriage with a non-Jewish partner, 2) mar- riage between a man and an already married woman, 3) incestuous mar- riage prohibited in the Bible. This category is extended to include a marriage between a man and his grandmothers-in-law. (The prohibition against marrying the wife of one's father's brother applies whether that brother is or is not from the same father. However, in the latter case the marriage takes effect and therefore falls into the category of prohibited but valid.)

The cases in this category do not require a divorce since the marriage act *Divorce* is entirely without consequence. An exception was made in the case of a marriage performed between a man and an already married woman in which case both her "husbands" are required to divorce her; the first because his wife committed adultery and the second as a *takkanah* lest people, under the mistaken impression that his marriage was valid, come to believe that a marriage can be terminated without a *get*.

Of late there has been a tendency among some Reform rabbis to officiate *Reform* at wedding ceremonies in which one of the parties is a non-Jew who has

85

not undergone conversion (even according to Reform practice) to Judaism. This tendency has been the cause of intense agitation within the Reform movement and some leaders of that movement have come out strongly against it.

Marriages, Prohibited but Valid

In this category are included marriages which, although prohibited, do not constitute incest according to biblical law, and therefore are valid and not terminable unless by death of either party or by divorce. Since these marriages are nevertheless prohibited and remain tainted with the prohibition during their subsistence, their dissolution by divorce is generally compelled, whether or not either or both of the parties consented to, or had prior knowledge of, the true situation. Marriage prohibitions of this kind derive either from the pentateuchal law or from rabbinic enactment.

The following are examples of such prohibitions: 1) Incestuous marriages of a minor degree (not expressly written in the Bible), such as a man with his grandmothers, his grandfather's wife or his wife's stepmother. Similarly, a man is prohibited from marrying his great-granddaughters, his grandson's wife or his mother's brother's wife (see chart, page 82–83). *Incestuous Marriage*

2) A married woman who has sexual relations with anyone but her husband of her own free will, becomes prohibited to her husband (and lover) forever. If she had been raped, she is prohibited to her husband only if he is a *kohen*. *Adultery*

In the Bible a special ceremony is ordained for cases in which the husband suspects his wife of adultery but has no witnesses to it. This ceremony, known as the Ordeal of Jealousy, was conducted by a *kohen* within the Temple confines and was intended to "prove" whether or not she had committed adultery. *Ordeal of Jealousy*

The suspected woman was required to bring a meal offering consisting of barley without its usual oil and frankincense addition. The *kohen* took

Parchment *ketubbah,* Modena, Italy, 1757. The outer margin is decorated with the signs of the Zodiac, while the inner one is framed by a micrographic script comprising passages from the Song of Songs, Ecclesiastes, and Proverbs.

"Jewish Wedding" by Moritz Oppenheimer, 1861. A *tallit* serves as the *ḥuppah* and the bride and groom are joined by wedding belts. Note the *traustein* in the synagogue wall and the *badḥan* at the top of the steps.

some Temple water in a vessel and sprinkled some earth from the Temple floor into it. He then uncovered the head of the woman and placed the meal offering in her hands while he held the bitter waters. An oath was then administered that she was not guilty of any of the accusations brought by her husband on penalty of severe physical changes occurring in her body, to which she replied that she was not guilty. The *kohen* then wrote the oath, which incorporated the Divine Name, on parchment and dipped the scroll into the water until the lettering was erased. The woman drank the water and the sacrifice of the meal offering by the *kohen* ended the ceremony.

If nothing happened to the woman she was "proven" to be innocent and was assured of some compensation for the indignity she has suffered. According to one interpretation in the Talmud, if she has been hitherto barren she would now be able to conceive; whereas according to another her barrenness would not be cured but if she had had children previously, her future offspring would be superior.

The rabbis of the Talmud stressed the moral to be drawn from this ceremony: so much does the Almighty cherish marital peace that He allows His Holy Name to be irradicated in order to save it.

In post-Temple times when it was no longer possible to perform the ceremony, a serious, grounded suspicion on the part of the husband that his wife had committed adultery resulted in his being forbidden to cohabit with her and he was required to divorce her.

3) A divorcée who had remarried and whose second marriage has also been terminated (by divorce or death) is prohibited to her former husband. *Remarriage*

4) A *kohen* may not marry a divorcée, a *zonah,* or a *halalah.* A divorced woman remains prohibited to a *kohen* even if after her divorce she had married and subsequently become a widow. A *kohen* is forbidden to remarry even his own former wife. For the purposes of the above prohibition, the term *zonah* is not to be interpreted in its ordinary sense—i.e., a woman who has sexual relations other than within matrimony. Here *Kohen*

87

it refers to a woman who is not a Jewess by birth, such as a proselyte, and also to a woman who has cohabited with a man to whom she must not be married by virtue of a general prohibition (i.e., not one relating to the priesthood as such), e.g., if she cohabited with a non-Jew or a *mamzer*. Should the *kohen* have sexual relations with either a divorcée or a *zonah*, that woman, immediately after the first intercourse, becomes a *halalah* and from then is prohibited to the *kohen* on two accounts. A female child born of this union is also a *halalah* and may not marry a *kohen*, but her children (of a legitimate marriage) are as any legitimate Jewish stock and may marry freely. The male child born of such an illegitimate union is a *halal* and has none of the privileges of the priesthood. In turn his male offspring retain his blemish throughout the generations but his female offspring are similar to the female offspring mentioned above.

5) Marriage with a divorcée or a widow is prohibited before the lapse of *Paternity* ninety days from the date of her acquiring her new status, in order to avoid doubt concerning the paternity of her offspring; similarly, for the good of her child, it is forbidden to marry a pregnant woman or a nursing mother until the child has reached the age of twenty-four months.

6) A Jewish man or woman must not marry a *mamzer*, i.e., a person born *Mamzer* of an incestuous or adulterous union. The children of such a marriage are themselves *mamzerim*. A marriage between two *mamzerim*, as well as a male or female *mamzer* with a male or female proselyte, is permitted, the children remaining *mamzerim*. However, since the offspring of a union between a Jew and a gentile takes the status of the mother, a child born of a *mamzer* and a gentile mother will be a gentile and not a *mamzer*, thus after proper conversion to Judaism, the child would acquire the status of a legitimate proselyte, and the fact that his father was a *mamzer* will be wholly irrelevant.

Sometimes there may be a doubt about the status of a child, e.g., a child *"Doubtful"* found abandoned in a public place, when the identity of neither parent *Mamzer* is known, and therefore the child has the status of "doubtful" *mamzer*.

88

As such, he cannot marry either a legitimate Jewess (because he may be a *mamzer*) or a female *mamzer* (because he may in fact not be a *mamzer*), or another "doubtful" *mamzer*. He, however, may marry a proselyte, the children of that marriage remaining "doubtful" *mamzerim*.

Halakhic problems concerning a "doubtful" *mamzer* have arisen in con- *Karaites* nection with the Karaites because, while their marriage may be valid according to Jewish law, their method of divorce is not. Accordingly, a Karaite woman who is divorced according to Karaite law is in essence not divorced and any child she bears to another man whom she marries is then a *mamzer*. Since it is impossible to determine who, throughout the generations, remarried on the strength of such an invalid divorce, Jewish law casts the suspicion of "doubtful" *mamzer* on all members of that community. However, some scholars did permit marriage with Karaites on the grounds that even their marriages are not in accordance with Jewish law as they lack qualified witnesses. In this latter opinion, no stigma of *mamzerut* is to be attached to a child of a Karaite woman who married, was divorced and then married another man, all in accordance with Karaite rites only, since—in Jewish law—she is regarded as never having been married at all.

In the 1950's and 1960's it was suggested that such a doubt existed about *Benei Israel* a community of Indian Jews, the Benei Israel, the majority of whose members had immigrated to the State of Israel. A great amount of literature, some of it of a polemical nature, was written on the subject and members of the community even held demonstrations in Jerusalem. The problem was solved finally by the Israel Rabbinate's decision that the doubt did not exist in this case.

7) Marriages of two brothers or two sisters are not performed on the same day in order not to mix the joyousness of one occasion with that of another.

In each of the prohibited but valid marriages either party is entitled to *Demanding* demand a divorce, whether or not either or both parties were aware of *a Divorce* the impediment at the time of the marriage or at any time thereafter. **89**

In case of the other party's refusal, divorce may be compelled, except in the case of a marriage contracted within ninety days of dissolution of the wife's previous marriage. The need for divorce is also relaxed with reference to marriage with a pregnant woman or nursing mother, and marriage of brothers or sisters on the same day.

Monogamy vs. Polygamy

The Bible does not limit the right of a man to have more than one wife. *In the* Indeed, many instances can be cited (including the Patriarchs) where a *Bible* man had several wives (and concubines)—a prevalent custom in the ancient Near East. However, practice was more monogamous than theory. Psalms and Proverbs seem to take it for granted that a man had only one wife. The prophets, as well, using marriage as a metaphor for God's attachment to Israel, clearly have monogamous marriage in mind, since God did not enter into such a relationship with any other people.

Despite the rare occurrence of polygamy, its explicit prohibition in the *Origin of* laws of the Dead Sea Sect that saw polygamy as a pentateuchal pro- *Monogamy* hibition was a complete innovation. Christianity adopted a similar attitude, which was in conformity with Jesus' approach to marriage and to divorce.

Although most of the mishnaic and talmudic literature reflect a tendency *In the* toward monogamy, polygamy did continue to exist. The *amora* Rava *Talmud* said: "A man may marry several women, on condition that he can provide for them." The sages also advised that one should not take more than four wives (which might be the source of Muslim law which permits only four wives).

Indeed polygamy was practiced among North African and Spanish Jews (Sephardim), while to the Ashkenazi Jews in Germany and France, mainly due to the economic conditions and to the influence of the Christian environment, monogamy became the rule.

In the course of time and for varying reasons, it became apparent that *Rabbinical* there was a need for the enactment of a general prohibition against *Enactment* polygamy. Accordingly, relying on the principle of endeavouring to prevent matrimonial strife (which principle had already been well developed in talmudic law) a regulation was enacted which is attributed to Rabbi *Herem de-* Gershom ben Judah (c. 960–1028) and his court prohibiting a man from *Rabbenu* marrying an additional wife unless specifically permitted to do so on special grounds by at least one hundred rabbis from three different countries. This regulation, known as ḥerem de-Rabbenu Gershom, also prohibited a husband from divorcing his wife against her will.

Since the prohibition against polygamy is derived from this regulation and not from any undertaking given by the husband to his wife, she is not competent to agree to a waiver of its application, lest she be subjected to undue influence by her husband. Nevertheless, if the husband does enter into a further marriage it will be considered legally valid, but as a prohibited marriage, and the first wife can require the court to compel the husband to divorce the other woman. Since the first wife cannot be obliged to live with a "rival," she may also ask that the court order (but not compel) the husband to give her (i.e., the first wife) a divorce. If the husband divorces his first wife, he is then released from his obligation to divorce his second wife, although his marriage to her in the first place was in defiance of the prohibition.

This regulation did not extend to those countries where it was apparent *Acceptance* that it had never been accepted. In general, as was noted before, the *of Enactment* regulation was accepted as binding among Ashkenazi communities, but not among the Sephardi and Oriental communities. In practice, therefore, Oriental communities would customarily insert an express provision in the *ketubbah,* whereby the husband was precluded from taking an additional wife except with the consent of his first wife or with the permission of the courts.

People who move from a country where the regulation is binding to a country where it is not, or vice versa, remain or become subject to it from thenceforth. However, if a man legally married two wives in a country where this was permitted, he is not obliged to divorce either woman on arriving in another country where the regulation is in force, as the law is only infringed upon by his taking an additional wife.

The State of Israel has enacted a law making monogamy binding upon all Jews irrespective of their communal affiliations. This, however, does not render a second marriage invalid according to biblical law, and therefore, if such a marriage does take place, it can be absolved only by death or divorce. The criminal law of the State, however, renders it an offense on pain of imprisonment for a married person to contract another marriage. Nevertheless, for Jewish citizens no offense is committed if permission to marry a second wife is given by a final judgement of a rabbinical court and approved by the two chief rabbis of Israel.

Monogamy in the State of Israel

The object of prohibiting bigamy is to prevent a man from marrying a second wife as long as he is not legally entitled to dissolve his first marriage. Thus, in order to avoid any circumvention of the prohibition, the regulation also generally prohibits divorce against the will of the wife. This double prohibition may, however, result in the husband being unjustifiably fettered in circumstances where he would not otherwise be required by law to maintain his ties with his wife—and yet may not divorce her against her will. This can, therefore, be obviated by the availability of a "release" from the regulation against bigamy, which is granted by the court in the appropriate circumstances. This "release" does not mean that the first wife is divorced, but that the husband is granted exceptional permission to contract an additional marriage. Naturally, such a step is taken only if the court, after a full investigation of the relevant facts, is satisfied that a release is legally justified, and after one hundred rabbis from three different countries have agreed. Thus, for example, a "release" would be granted in a case where a wife becomes insane. Her husband cannot, therefore, maintain normal married life with her, a fact which would ordinarily entitle him to divorce her; this he cannot do because of her legal incapacity. Similarly, a man may obtain a "release" if his wife refuses to accept a divorce, despite a court order that she do so (e.g., in the case of prohibited but valid incestuous marriages).

"Release" from Enactment

Civil Marriage

Since in Jewish law a woman is not considered a wife unless she has *Divorce* been married in accordance with Jewish law, any marriage celebrated *Requirement* according to secular law alone should not carry with it any legal stigma and therefore, the parties to a civil marriage should not require a Jewish divorce. However, because it is a talmudic rule that a "Jew does not live licentiously when he is able to live according to the *mitzvah*," and although today it is punishable by flogging, a man could effect a marriage by sexual intercourse. Authorities discuss the possibility that a husband and wife, by virtue of a civil ceremony, might require a divorce out of strictness, i.e., lest the public (who might consider this couple as man and wife by Jewish law) conclude that any such man and wife could each contract another marriage with another party without first having been divorced from each other.

Some authorities argue that the mere fact that the civilly-married couple are living together does not constitute a Jewish marriage by intercourse, inasmuch as the latter means sexual relations between the parties expressly for the sake of *kiddushin*, whereas cohabitation is taking place not to establish marriage but rather by virtue of a marriage already celebrated. These scholars also reject the idea of effecting a divorce—lest the public go astray—because, on the contrary, the giving of a bill of divorce may create the impression that a civil ceremony creates a matrimonial tie, which it does not.

The above dispute stems essentially from the fact that on the one hand a *Application* civil marriage is an indication by the parties of their disinterest in a Jewish marriage, yet on the other hand, the surrounding circumstances may sometimes leave room for doubt as to whether the requirements of a Jewish marriage had not been fulfilled nevertheless. Hence the legal status of the parties requires determination according to the circumstances in each case, with particular regard to the legal system, social background and degree of freedom pertaining to the celebration of marriage prevailing in the country concerned. In countries with no restriction on the celebration of marriages in accordance with Jewish law, the absence of such a ceremony can be considered an indication of the parties to marry only by secular law. Therefore, no divorce will be required. In contrast, however, a civil ceremony celebrated in a country where the celebration of a Jewish marriage might bring the parties into danger, and it can be assumed that, but for the danger the parties would have had a religious ceremony (by virtue of the presumption against "licentious living"), a divorce out of strictness will be required.

Child Marriage

A rare form of marriage today is child marriage. A male is legally a minor (child) until the end of his thirteenth year. A female is a minor until the end of her twelfth year; thereafter she is considered an adult—but with one additional distinction: for the first six months after her twelfth birthday she is called a *na'arah*.

A bride of 12, with her husband in Morocco, 1953.

94

In Jewish law a minor cannot execute the act of marriage. In the case of a male minor, the rule is that no one can contract a marriage for him, and thus only at the age of thirteen and one day may he himself marry. With a female minor, on the other hand, the father may contract a marriage for her until she is twelve years and six months old. She herself may contract a marriage during the six-month period that she is a *na'arah* only with prior permission of her father.

In the State of Israel steps have been taken to prevent child marriages. By *State of* an enactment adopted by the National Rabbinical Conference held in *Israel* Jerusalem in 1950, a man is forbidden to contract a marriage with a girl under the age of sixteen, nor may her father give her in marriage. However, this prohibition does not nullify a marriage that has nonetheless been celebrated in defiance of it, since in Jewish law such a marriage may be valid. Under the Marriage Age Law, 1950, as amended in 1960, it is an offense punishable by imprisonment or fine or both for any person to marry a girl under the age of seventeen or to celebrate or assist in the celebration of such a marriage in any capacity (e.g., as rabbi or cantor) or for a father, guardian, or relative to give the girl away in marriage.

12. DOCUMENTS

Presented here are various documents connected with marriage and its termination. The documents, which are given in their original forms and in free translation, are couched in Jewish legal formulae which are quite ancient, being, for the most part, found in the Talmud. Like all legal formulae they are designed to be very exact; to the lay reader, however, they can appear to be very complicated. All the documents have been referred to in the body of the text above.

Form of Ketubbah

On the (first) day of the week, the . . . . . . day of the month . . . ., in the year five thousand, six hundred and . . . . . . since the creation of the world, the era according to which we are accustomed to reckon here in the city of (name of city, state and country), how (name of bridegroom), son of (name of father), surnamed (family name), said to this virgin (name of bride), daughter of (name of father), surnamed (family name): "Be thou my wife according to the law of Moses and Israel, and I will cherish, honor, support and maintain thee in accordance with the custom of Jewish husbands who cherish, honor, support and maintain their wives in truth. And I herewith make for thee the settlements of virgins, two hundred silver zuzim, which belongs to thee, according to the law of Moses and Israel; and (I will also give thee) food, clothing and necessaries, and live with thee as husband and wife according to universal custom." And Miss (name of bride), this virgin, consented and became his wife. The wedding outfit that she brought unto him from her father's house, in silver, gold, valuables, wearing apparel, house furniture, and bedclothes, all this (name of bridegroom), the said bridegroom, accepted in the sum of one hundred silver pieces, and (name of bridegroom), the bridegroom, consented to increase this amount from his own property with the sum of one hundred silver pieces, making in all two hundred silver pieces. And thus said (name of bridegroom), the bridegroom: "The responsibility of this marriage contract, of this wedding outfit, and of this additional sum, I take upon myself and my heirs after me, so that they shall be paid from the best part of my property and possession that I have beneath the whole heaven, that which I now possess or may hereafter acquire. All my property, real and personal, even the mantle on my shoulders, shall be mortgaged to secure the payment of this marriage contract, of the wedding outfit, and of the addition made thereto, during my lifetime and after my death, from the present day and forever." (Name of bridegroom), the bridegroom, has taken upon himself the responsibility of this marriage contract, of the wedding outfit and the addition made thereto, according to the restrictive usages of all marriage contracts and the additions thereto made for the daughters of Israel, in accordance with the institution of our sages of blessed memory. It is not to be regarded as a mere forfeiture without consideration or as a mere formula of a document. We have followed the legal formality of symbolic delivery (*kinyan*) between (name of bridegroom), the son of . . . . . . the bridegroom, and (name of bride), the daughter of . . . . . ., this virgin, and we have used a garment legally fit for the purpose, to strengthen all that is stated above, AND EVERYTHING IS VALID AND CONFIRMED.

Attested to . . . . . . (Witness)
Attested to . . . . . . (Witness)

Form of Tenaim

TO GOOD FORTUNE

MAY IT COME UP AND SPROUT FORTH LIKE A GREEN GARDEN.
WHOSO FINDS A WIFE FINDS A GREAT GOOD, AND OBTAINS
FAVOR OF THE GOOD LORD, WHO RATIFIES THIS UNION.

May He who predestinates, bestow a good name and future to the provisions embodied in this agreement, which were agreed upon by the two parties hereto, that is, as party of the first part, Mr. . . . . , who represents the groom Mr. . . . . . . , and as party of the second part, Mr. . . . . , who represents the bride Miss . . . .

Firstly: That the above named groom agrees to take himself as wife the above named bride, through *huppah* and betrothal, in accordance with the Law of Moses and Israel; that they will neither abstract nor conceal from one another any property whatsoever, but they shall equally have power over their property, pursuant to the established custom.

The above named groom obligates himself to present the bride with gifts according to custom.

The above named bride obligates herself to give as her dowry the sum of . . . . . . in cash, and clothes, pillows and linens, as is the custom.

The wedding will take place, if the Almighty so wills it, on the . . . . . . day of . . . . . . in the year . . . . . . or sooner than such date or later if both parties agree thereto.

A fine is to be paid, by the party breaking this agreement, to the other party, in the fixed sum of . . . . . . and also in accordance with the law of the land.

All of the foregoing was done with perfect understanding and due deliberation, and by means of the most effective method, in accordance with the ordinance of the sages, of blessed memory, and in accordance with the law of the land; by means of striking hands, by solemn promises, by true affirmation, by handing over an object (from one contracting party to another), to take effect immediately; and this is not to be regarded as a mere forfeiture without consideration, or as a mere formula of a document. We have followed the legal formality of a symbolic delivery *(kinyan)*, by handing over an object, between the groom and the bride and their representatives, by using a garment legally fit for the purpose, to validate all that is stated above,

AND EVERYTHING IS VALID AND CONFIRMED.

For the further purpose of making this agreement binding and obligatory, the groom and the bride themselves have attached their signatures hereunto this . . . . . . day of . . . . . . , in the year . . . . . . at . . . . . . (name of town).

Attested to . . . . . . (Groom)
Attested to . . . . . . (Bride)

In our presence, the undersigned witnesses, did the above named groom and bride attach their signatures, to affirm all that is stated above, and in our presence did they go through the legal formality of symbolic delivery, by handing over an object from one party to the other (*kinyan*), that this agreement take effect immediately; and we have verified and affirmed it as is required by law.

In witness whereof, we have hereunto set our hands this . . . . . . day of . . . . . . in the year . . . . . . at . . . . . . (name of town).

Attested to . . . . . . (Witness)
Attested to . . . . . . (Witness)

*Ketubbah de'Irchesa

This happened before us on the . . . . . . day of week, the . . . . . . day of the month of . . . . . . in the year . . . . . . according to the era which we are accustomed to reckon here in the city . . . . How . . . . . . the son of . . . . . . came before us and declared: "This woman, ... the daughter of . . . . . . was originally married to me as wife when she was a virgin in the town of . . . . . . according to the laws of Jewish women who are married to their husbands by *ḥuppah*, betrothal and with a *ketubbah*.

She has lost her *ketubbah* document which was written for her from the day she was married to me and since the rabbis have said that a Jew may not live with his wife even for one hour without a *ketubbah*, I now desire to write her another *ketubbah* in place of the first *ketubbah* with its dowry and additional sum."

Therefore, we, the undersigned witnesses, have now made an act of acquisition from his because the first witnesses who signed the first *ketubbah* that was lost are not available and we do not know the date of that *ketubbah* and we have

98

written this *ketubbah* for her as a substitute for the first *ketubbah,* from this day and in the form in which, he has told us, the first *ketubbah,* which was lost, was written:

How . . . . . . the son of . . . .

Here follows the usual Ketubbah formula

We have followed the legal formality of acquisition between . . . . . . son of . . . . . . and . . . . . . the daughter of . . . . . . who was a virgin when she was married to him originally according to everything that is stated above with a garment that is legally fit for acquisition.

. . . . . . (witness)

. . . . . . (witness)

*This *ketubbah* is written when the original has been lost or destroyed (see page 36).

*Commitment to Grant Ḥaliẓah if Necessary

A record of evidence that took place before us the undersigned witnesses.

On the . . . . . . day of the week, the . . . . . . day of the month of . . . . . ., five thousand . . . . . . years since the creation of the world, the era according to which we are accustomed to reckon here in the city of . . . . . ., the brother . . . . . . came before us and said to us: "Be valid and faithful witnesses for me and accept a complete acquisition from me to the effect that I accept (the contents of this document) on myself completely and absolutely by the most solemn oath from which I can never be absolved except by permission of my brother's wife . . . . . . who shall own this document. And write it (the document) in every formula of attorney in every legally valid manner and sign it and give it to . . . . . . who is my brother's wife that it should be in her hand as evidence, attorney and proof that I agree out of my own good will and without any compulsion at all but with complete will and in perfect knowledge—and I make this statement before you as one who makes a declaration before an important court of law, i.e., an absolute statement valid and confirmed which cannot be retracted from this day henceforth:

That if, God forbid, my brother . . . . . . the husband of . . . . . . should die without issue and his wife . . . . . . will thus need *haliẓah* then when she shall require me to grant her *haliẓah* I will be liable to free her by a valid *haliẓah*—gratis, and I shall not take from her nor from anybody else for her even the smallest sum of money in the world, immediately after three months will have passed since the death of my abovementioned brother, God forbid; at which time she can receive *halizah,* on condition that she shall come to me. As long as I shall not grant her *halizah* as above, my sister-in-law shall be maintained at my expense.

And if . . . . . . requires me to free her by a valid *halizah* as above and I do not do so within six months from the demand I hereby commit myself to pay to my brother's wife . . . . . . the sum of . . . . . . pounds sterling for the delay."

All this above, the aforementioned . . . . . . accepted on himself by the most solemn oath and thereby cancelled any contrary declaration he may have made and invalidated any witnesses to any such declaration by all formulas of cancellation that the rabbis consider valid.

This *Halizah* document can never be contested in any way but shall always be interpreted to the benefit of its holder (the sister-in-law) whose claim shall be superior and the claim of the contestant inferior.

This document shall be as valid as if it had been written in an important court and is not to be regarded as a mere forfeiture without consideration or as a mere formula of a document.

We have followed the legal formality of acquisition between the brother . . . . . . and his brother's wife . . . . . . and we have used a garment legally fit for the purpose to strengthen all that is stated above.

. . . . . . (witness)
. . . . . . (witness)

This is the document that was used in London, England.

Get

On the . . . . . . day of the week, the . . . . . . day of the month of . . . . . . , in the year . . . . . . from the creation of the world according to the calendar reckoning we are accustomed to count here, in the city . . . . . . (which is also known as . . . . . .), which is located on the river . . . . . . (and on the river . . . . . .), and situated near wells of water, I, ... (also known as . . . . . .), the son of . . . . . . (also known as . . . . . .), who today am present in the city . . . . . . (which is also known as . . . . . .), which is located on the river . . . . . . (and on the

100

river . . . . . .), and situated near wells of water, do willingly consent, being under no restraint, to release, to set free, and put aside thee, my wife, ... (also known as . . . . . .), daughter of . . . . . . (also known as . . . . . .), who art today in the city of . . . . . . (which is also known as . . . . . .), which is located on the river . . . . . . (and on the river . . . . . .), and situated near wells of water, who has been my wife from before. Thus do I set free, release thee, and put thee aside, in order that thou may have permission and the authority over thyself to go and marry any man thou may desire. No person may hinder thee from this day onward, and thou are permitted to every man. This shall be for thee from me a bill of dismissal, a letter of release and a document of freedom, in accordance with the laws of Moses and Israel.

. . . . . . the son of . . . . . . , witness
. . . . . . the son of . . . . . ., witness

Gargush. Hood worn by Jewish women of San'a, Yemen,
as part of bridal costume, late 19th century.

Kimpetbriefel, a protective amulet for a woman in childbirth, 18th century, East Europe. The text includes Psalm 121.

Agunah, woman unable to remarry according to Jewish law, because of desertion or inability to accept presumption of death.

Amora, title given to the Jewish scholars in Erez Israel and Babylonia in the third to sixth centuries.

Ashkenazi (pl. Ashkenazim), German or West-, Central-, or East-European Jew(s), as contrasted with Sephardi.

Av, fifth month of the Jewish religious year, eleventh of the civil, approximating to July–August.

Bi'ah, the sexual act.

Birkat Erusin, betrothal benediction.

Birkot Nissu'in, marriage benedictions.

Day of Atonement, tenth day of the month of Tishrei (September–October), most solemn day of the Jewish year.

Erusin, betrothal ceremony.

Get, bill of divorce.

Halakhah, Jewish law.

Halizah, ceremony performed when a man refuses to marry his brother's widow when that brother died childless.

Hanukkah, eight-day celebration starting the twenty-fifth day of the month of Kislev (November–December) commemorating the victory of Judah Maccabee over the Syrian king Antiochus Epiphanes and the subsequent rededication of the Temple.

Hazzan, precentor who intones the liturgy and leads the prayer in the synagogue.

Herem, excommunication; ban.

Huppah, nuptial canopy.

Iyyar, eighth month of the Jewish religious year, second of the civil, approximating to April–May.

Ketubbah, marriage contract, stipulating husband's obligations to wife.

Kiddushin, betrothal ceremony.

Kohen (pl. *Kohanim*), Jew(s) of priestly (Aaronide) descent.

Lag ba-Omer, thirty-third day of the *omer* period falling on the eighteenth day of the month of Iyyar; a semi-holiday.

Mamzer (pl. *Mamzerim*), bastard, according to Jewish law, the offspring of an incestuous or adulterous relationship. *Mamzerut* is the state of being a *mamzer.*

Mikveh (pl. *Mikva'ot*), ritual bath.

Minyan, group of ten male adult Jews, the minimum required for communal prayer.

Mishnah, earliest codification of Jewish Oral Law, completed in the third century C.E.

Mitzvah, biblical or rabbinic injunction; applied also to good or charitable deeds.

Mohar, bride price.

Na'arah, a girl between the ages of twelve years and twelve years and six months.

Niddah, woman during the period of menstruation and until subsequent purification.

Nisan, first month of the Jewish religious year, seventh of the civil, approximating to March–April.

Nissu'in, marriage ceremony.

Omer, forty-nine days counted from the first sheaf cut during the barley harvest that was offered in the Temple (second day of Passover) until Shavuot.

Passover, a spring festival, beginning on the fifteenth of the month of Nisan, lasting seven days in Israel and eight days in the diaspora, commemorating the Exodus from Egypt.

Purim, festival held on the fourteenth or fifteenth of the month of Adar (February–March), commemorating the delivery of the Jews of Persia in the time of Esther.

Rosh ha-Shanah, two-day holiday at the beginning of the month of Tishrei (September–October), traditionally the New Year.

Rosh Hodesh, New Moon; first day of the Hebrew month.

Sephardi (pl. Sephardim), Jew(s) of Spain and Portugal and their descendants, wherever resident, as contrasted with Ashkenazi.

Shavuot, Pentecost, Feast of Weeks; celebrated one day in Israel and two days in the diaspora in the month of Sivan (May–June), commemorating the receiving of the Torah at Mount Sinai.

Shekhinah, Divine Presence.

Shetar, deed, contract.

Sheva Berakhot, seven benedictions of the marriage ceremony.

Shevat, eleventh month of the Jewish religious year, fifth of the civil, approximating to January–February.

Shiddukhin, engagement ceremony.

Sivlonot, pre-wedding gifts of the groom to the bride or *vice versa.*

Sukkot, Tabernacles, festival beginning on the fifteenth of the month of Tishrei (September–October).

104

Taharat ha-Mishpaḥah, family purity.

Takkanah, regulation supplementing the law of the Torah.

Tallit, prayer shawl.

Talmud, compendium of discussions on the Mishnah by generations of scholars and jurists in many academies over a period of several centuries.

Tammuz, fourth month of the Jewish religious year, tenth of the civil, approximating to June–July.

Tena'im, marriage conditions, sometimes written in a formal contract.

Yevamah, woman awaiting levirate marriage or *ḥalizah*.

Yiḥud, seclusion of bride and groom following marriage ceremony.

ABBREVIATIONS TO SOURCES

Bible

Gen.	—	Genesis	Jud.	—	Judges	Mal.	—	Malachi
Ex.	—	Exodus	Sam.	—	Samuel	Ps.	—	Psalms
Lev.	—	Leviticus	Is.	—	Isaiah	Prov.	—	Proverbs
Num.	—	Numbers	Ezek.	—	Ezekiel	Song.	—	Song of Songs
Deut.	—	Deuteronomy	Hos.	—	Hosea	Macc.	—	Maccabees

Talmud[1]

TJ—Jerusalem Talmud[2]

Av.Z.	—	*Avodah Zarah*	Ket.	—	*Ketubbot*	Pes.	—	*Pesaḥim*
BB.	—	*Bava Batra*	Kid.	—	*Kiddushin*	Sanh.	—	*Sanhedrin*
Ber.	—	*Berakhot*	Mak.	—	*Makkot*	Shab.	—	*Shabbat*
Bez.	—	*Beẓah*	Meg.	—	*Megillah*	Sof.	—	*Soferim*
BM.	—	*Bava Meẓia*	Mik.	—	*Mikva'ot*	Sot.	—	*Sotah*
Git.	—	*Gittin*	MK	—	*Mo'ed Katan*	Ta'an.	—	*Ta'anit*
Hul.	—	*Ḥulin*	Ned.	—	*Nedarim*	Yev.	—	*Yevamot*
Kel.	—	*Kelim*	Nid.	—	*Nidah*			

Later Authorities

Yad	—	Maimonides, *Yad Ḥazakah*
Sh.Ar.	—	*Shulḥan Arukh*
EH	—	*Even ha-Ezer*
HM	—	*Ḥoshen Mishpat*
OH	—	*Oraḥ Ḥayyim*
YD	—	*Yoreh De'ah*
PDR	—	*Piskei Din Shel Battei ha-Din ha-Rabbaniyyim be-Yisrael*

---

[1] References to the Mishnah are in the form Yev. 3:6 (i.e., tractate *Yevamot*, chapter 3, Mishnah 6); references to the Gemara are in the form Yev. 12b (i.e., tractate *Yevamot*, page 12 side b. Thus, a reference Kid. 3:5, 18a will first refer to the Mishnah and then to the Gemara.

[2] Otherwise Talmud references are to Babylonian Talmud.

106

SOURCES

1   "no man would build. . . ." — *Midrash Rabbah*, Gen. 9:7

1   "You shall be holy . . ." — Rashi to Lev. 19:2

2   husband's conjugal . . . frequency — Ket. 47b; *Sefer Mitzvot Katan*, no. 285; Pes. 72b

2   "He created it . . ." — Is. 45:18

2   "be fruitful . . ." — Gen. 1:28

2   Bet Shammai . . . Bet Hillel — Yev. 6:6

2   Onan — Gen. 38:8–10

2   irregular . . . sexual play — Ned. 20b; Yad, *Issurei Bi'ah* 21:9; Abraham David of Posquieres, *Ba'alei Hanefesh*, Sha'ar Ha-Kedushah.

3   "the abominations of Egypt" — Sifra 9:8

3   female clothing — Deut. 22:5

3   "Male and female . . .". . . — Gen. 1:27; Genesis Rabbah 8:1; see also Ber. 61a

4   spends . . . sinful thoughts — Kid. 29b

4   "is as if he shed blood . . ." — Sh.Ar., EH 1:1 based on Yev. 63b–64a

4   "and he will have . . . account . . ." — Shab. 31a

4   "He who has no wife . . ." — Yev. 62b

4   high priest — Yoma 1:1 based on Lev. 16:6, 11, 17

4   *hazzan* — Sh. Ar., OH 581:1

4   A story . . . Roman — *Midrash Rabbah*, Lev., 8:1

5   "and I will betroth . . . " — Hos. 2:21–22

6   "For as a young . . ." — Is. 62:5

6   sell a Torah Scroll — Meg. 27a; Sh.Ar., EH 1:2

6   woman will tolerate — Yev. 113a; Kid. 7a

6   not be for money — Kid. 70a

6   mild-tempered, tactful . . . — Sot. 3b

6   beauty — Ber. 57b; Yoma 74b

6   social background — Kid. 49a

6   age — Yev. 44a; Sanh. 76a–b

6   respectability of family — Ta'an. 4:8; BB 109b

6   scholarly father — Pes. 49b

6   gotten to know her — Kid. 41a

6   eighteen for marriage — Avot 5:21

6   courts of law force — Sh.Ar., EH 1:3

109

110

111

112

page

114

Encyclopedia Judaica, Jerusalem, 1972, under:
  Betrothal; Civil Marriage; Divorce; Dowry; Marriage; Marriages, Prohibited

Abrahams, Israel, *Jewish Life in the Middle Ages,* London, 1932
Amram, David Werner, *The Jewish Law of Divorce,* Philadelphia, 1896
Aronson, David, *The Jewish Way of Life,* New York, 1946
Borowitz, Eugene B., *Choosing a Sex Ethic,* New York, 1969
Elman, Peter (ed.), *Jewish Marriage,* London, 1967
Epstein, Isidore, *The Jewish Way of Life,* London, 1946
Epstein, Louis M., *The Jewish Marriage Contract,* New York, 1927
—, *Marriage Laws in the Bible and the Talmud,* Cambridge, Mass., 1942
—, *Sex Laws and Customs in Judaims,* New York, 1948
Falk, Ze'ev Wilhelm, *Jewish Matrimonial Law in the Middle Ages,* London, 1966
Feldman, David M., *Birth Control in Jewish Law,* New York, 1968
Freid, Jacob (ed.), *Jews and Divorce,* New York, 1968
Gaster, Moses, *The Samaritans,* London, 1925
Goodman, Philip and Hanna, *The Jewish Marriage Anthology,* Philadelphia, 1965
Jakobovitz, Immanuel, *Jewish Medical Ethics,* New York, 1959, 1962
—, *Order of the Jewish Marriage Service,* New York, 1959
Kahana, Kopel, *The Theory of Marriage in Jewish Law,* London, 1966
Lamm, Norman, *A Hedge of Roses,* New York, 1966
Mace, David Robert, *Hebrew Marriage: A Sociological Study,* London, 1953
Maybaum, Ignaz, *The Jewish Home,* London, 1946
Mielziner, Moses, *The Jewish Law of Marriage and Divorce,* New York, 1901
Miller, David, *The Secret of the Jew,* Oakland, Calif., 1930
Neufeld, Ephraim, *Ancient Hebrew Marriage Laws,* London, 1944
Patai, Raphael, *Sex and Family in the Bible and the Middle East,* Garden City, New York, 1949
Rabinowitz, Mordechai (ed.), *Daughter of Israel,* New York, 1949
Rubens, Alfred, *A History of Jewish Costume,* New York, London, 1967
Schauss, Hayyim, *The Lifetime of a Jew,* Cincinnati, 1950

ILLUSTRATION CREDITS

COLOR CREDITS